Thunder Bay, Ontario Book 1 (Port Arthur Book 1), in Colour Photos, Saving Our History One Photo at a Time

Photography
by Barbara Raué
2017

Series Name:
Cruising Ontario

Book 173: Thunder Bay
(Port Arthur Book 1)

Cover photo: Red River Road, Queen Anne style – Page 21

Series Name: Cruising Ontario
Saving Our History One Photo at a Time
in colour photos

Books Available in Alphabetical Order:
Aberfoyle, Acton, Alton, Amherstburg, Ancaster, Arthur, Aylmer, Ayr, Bloomingdale, Brantford, Burlington, Caledon, Caledonia, Cambridge, Clifford, Conestogo, Delhi, Dorchester to Aylmer, Drayton, Drumbo, Dryden, Dundas, Eden Mills, Elmira, Elora, Essex, Fergus, Guelph, Hagersville, Hamilton, Hanover, Harriston, Hespeler, Jarvis, Kenora, Kingston, Kingsville, Kitchener, Linwood, Listowel, London, Lucknow, Midland, Mono, Mount Forest, Neustadt, New Hamburg, Niagara-on-the-Lake, Oakville, Orangeville, Orillia, Ottawa, Owen Sound, Palmerston, Penetanguishene, Peterborough, Petrolia, Port Elgin, Preston, Rockwood, Sarnia, Seaforth, Sheffield, Shelburne, Simcoe, Southampton, St. Jacobs, St. Marys, St. Thomas, Stoney Creek, Stratford, Thamesford, Tillsonburg, Waterdown, Waterford, Waterloo, Welland, Wellesley, Windsor, Wingham, Woodstock

Book 153: Kemptville
Book 154: Cornwall
Book 155: Mariatown to Maitland
Book 156: Morrisburg
Book 157: Brockville
Book 158: Merrickville
Book 159: Smiths Falls
Book 160: Portland, Newboro
Book 161: Westport & Area
Book 162: Perth
Book 163-166: Belleville
Book 167-168: Port Colborne
Book 169: Erin in Colour
Book 170: Goderich in Colour
Book 171: Sault Ste. Marie
Book 172: Lake Superior
Book 173-176: Thunder Bay

Other Books by Barbara Raue

Coins of Gold

Arrows, Indians and Love

The Life and Times of Barbara
Volume 1: Inventions That Have Enhanced My Life
Volume 2: Entertainment That I Have Enjoyed
Volume 3: East Coast Trips
Volume 4: Olympics Have Always Intrigued Me
Volume 5: Wonders of the World
Volume 6: Caribbean Cruises We Have Enjoyed
Volume 7: Animals
Volume 8: Storms and Other Major Disasters in My Lifetime
Volume 9: Wars, Terrorist Attacks and Major Disasters

The Cromwell Family Book

Laura Secord Discovered

Daddy Where Are You?

Montana Series
Book 1: Montana Dream
Book 2: Life on the Montana Frontier
Book 3: Montana to Boston and Back

Visit Barbara's website to view all of her books
http://barbararaue.ca

Table of Contents

Algoma Street South   Page 7

Waverley Street   Page 11

Red River Road   Page 17

Park Avenue   Page 25

Peter Street   Page 26

Hebert Street   Page 29

College Street   Page 31

Dufferin Street   Page 37

High Street   Page 38

Architectural Terms   Page 47

Building Styles   Page 52

Thunder Bay is a city in Northwestern Ontario. It is located on Lake Superior. European settlement in the region began in the late seventeenth century with a French fur trading outpost on the banks of the Kaministiquia River. It grew into an important transportation hub with its port forming an important link in the shipping of grain and other products from western Canada, through the Great Lakes and the Saint Lawrence Seaway, to the east coast. Forestry and manufacturing played important roles in the city's economy.

The city takes its name from the immense Thunder Bay at the head of Lake Superior, known on eighteenth-century French maps as *Baie du Tonnerre* (Bay of Thunder). The city is often referred to as the "Lakehead" because of its location at the end of Great Lakes navigation on the Canadian side of the border.

European settlement at Thunder Bay began with two French fur trading posts (1683, 1717) which were subsequently abandoned. In 1803, the Montreal-based North West Company established Fort William as its mid-continent post. The fort thrived until 1821 when the North West Company merged with the Hudson's Bay Company and Fort William was no longer needed.

By the 1850s, the Province of Canada began to take an interest in its western extremity. Discovery of copper in Michigan prompted a Canadian national demand for mining locations on the Canadian shores of Lake Superior. Another settlement developed a few miles to the north of Fort William with it eventually being called Port Arthur.

The arrival of the CPR in 1875 sparked a long rivalry between the towns, which did not end until the amalgamation of 1970. Until the 1880s, Port Arthur was a much larger and dynamic community. The CPR, in collaboration with the Hudson's Bay Company, preferred east Fort William, located on the lower Kaministiquia River where the fur trade posts were.

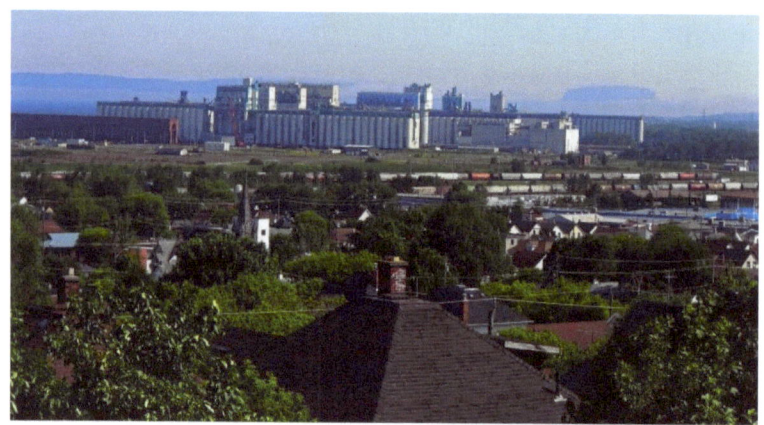

The Lakehead Terminal Grain Elevators

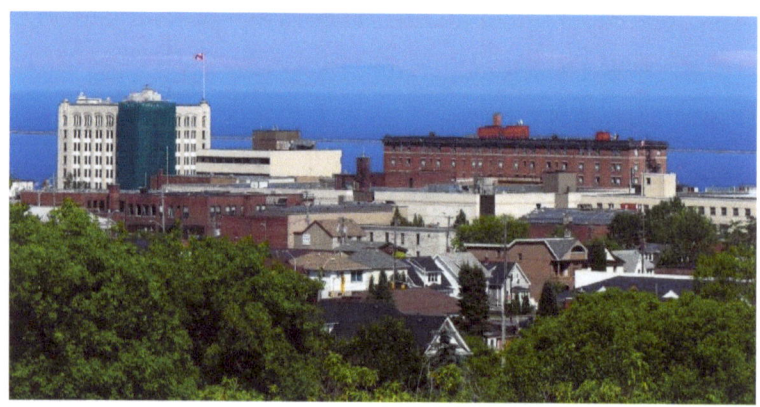

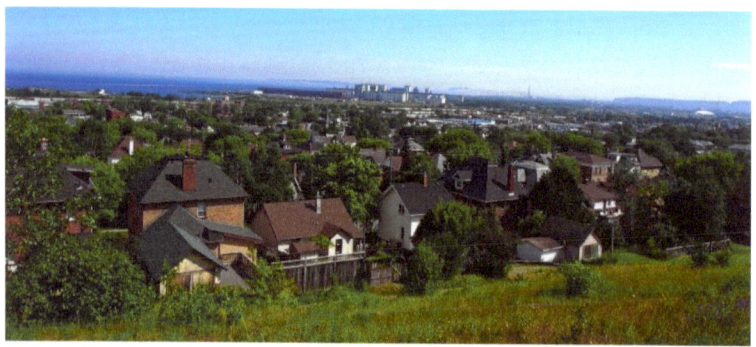

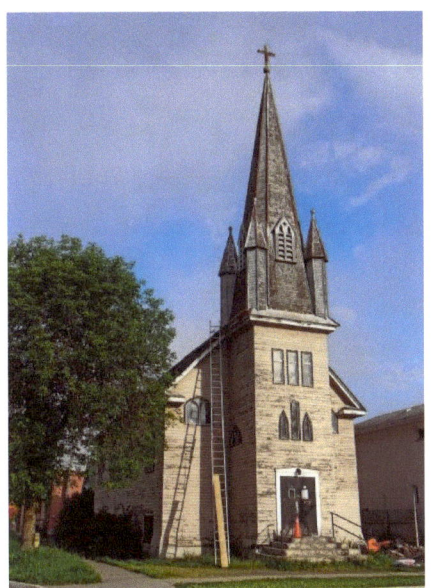
Finials around spire

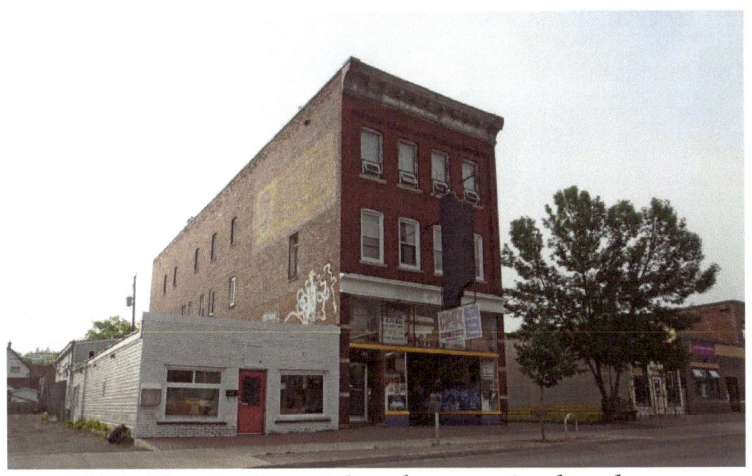
186 Algoma Street South – cornice brackets

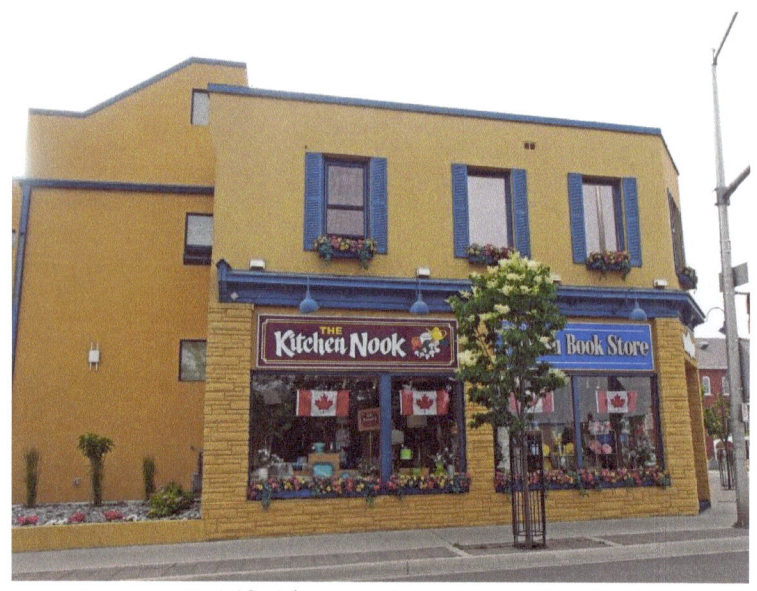

168 Algoma Street South

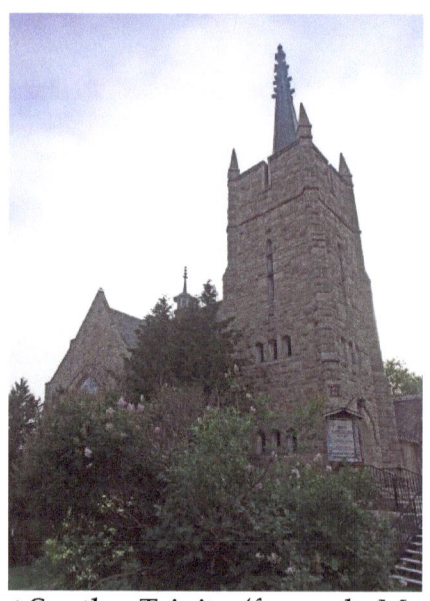

30 Algoma Street South – Trinity (formerly Methodist) United Church – 1906 – The building has very steeply pitched roofs and arched windows in the Late Gothic Revival style.

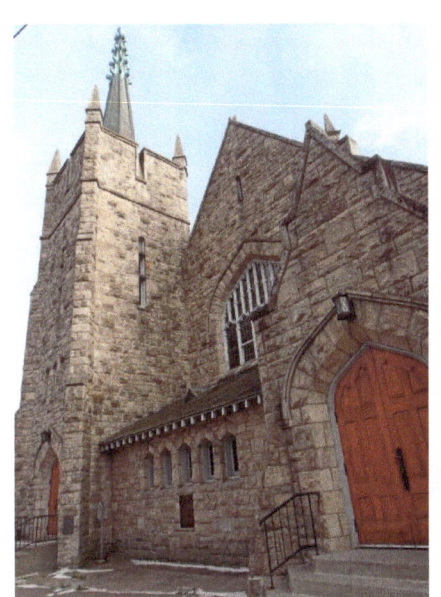 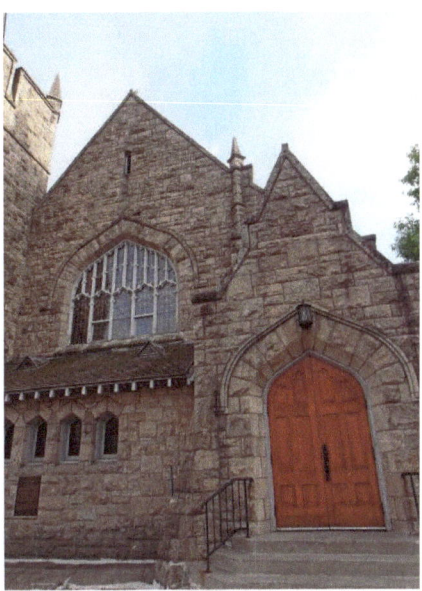

30 Algoma Street South – Trinity United Church - was constructed of rough cut stone. The tower features very narrow windows, four diagonal buttresses, each capped with a pyramid shaped pinnacle, and a very sharp hexagonal pinnacle-spire with crockets projecting from the tower roof. Between the windows and the battlements, there is a string course. An octagonal louvered cupola with a copper pinnacle is on the roof.

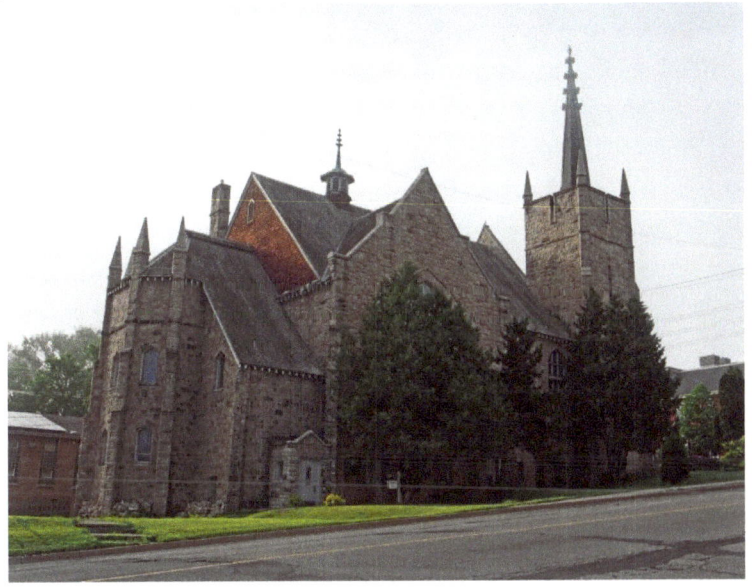

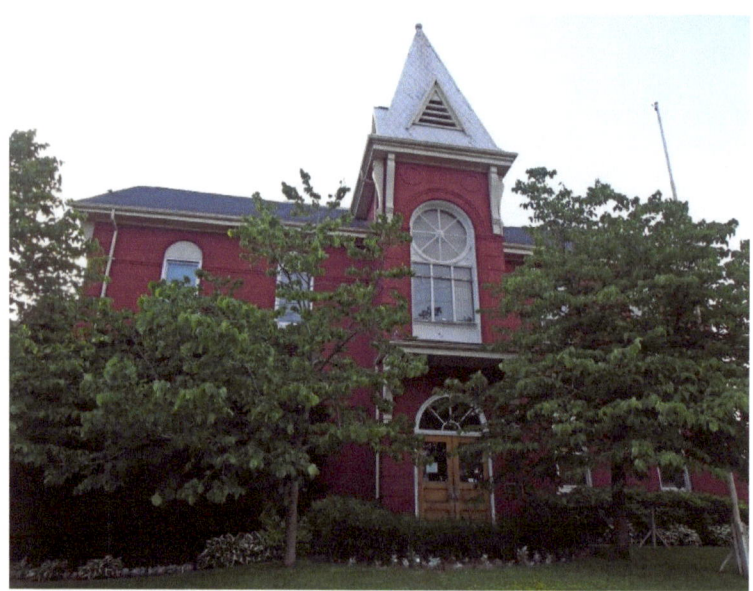

10 Algoma Street South – Central School was erected in 1884. In 1901 eight classrooms were added. It is the oldest remaining school building in the city and was used as a school until 1965.

The two-storey brick structure has a symmetrical façade dominated by a projecting central tower with a pyramidal roof and eaves supported by elongated wooden brackets. The tower has a large wheel window; a projecting shelf protects the entrance doors and fanlight. Brickwork on the tower is patterned with circles above the window wheel. The first floor windows have segmental arches while the second level windows are round-arched. A brick string course crosses the wall at each level. On the gable ends, the projecting eaves have triple wooden brackets at the eaves return.

Magnus Theatre, Thunder Bay's only professional theatre group, moved into the Central School building in 2001.

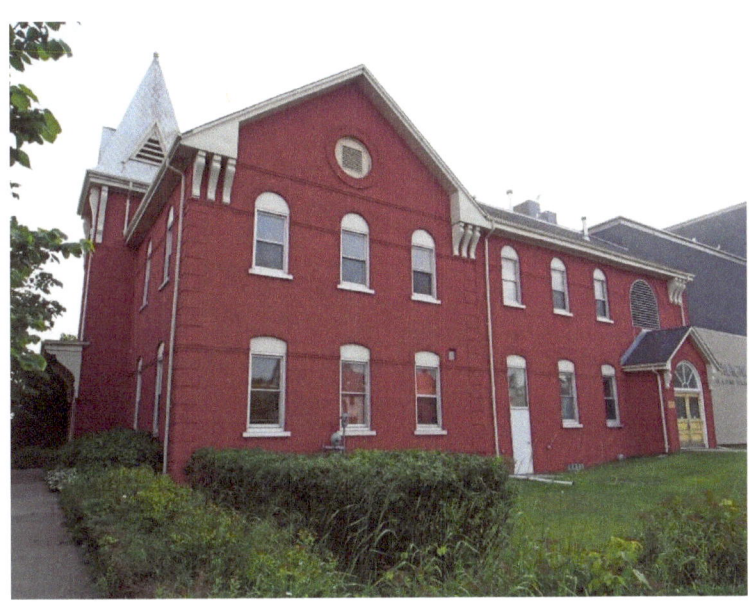

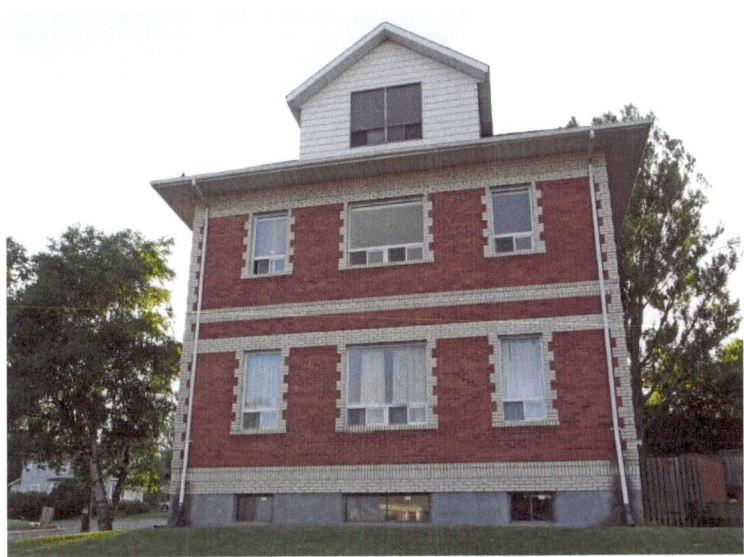

Waverley Street – dichromatic brickwork, dormer in roof

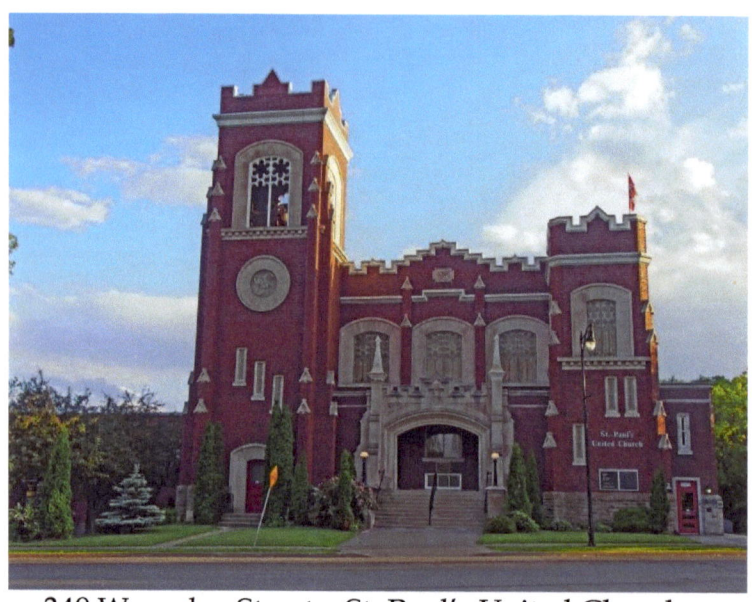

349 Waverley Street – St. Paul's United Church was built in 1914 in mixed styles of Georgian (stone window surrounds) and Late Gothic Revival (double towers, buttresses, and geometrical tracery). The façade appears complicated because of the two different towers, the arched entrance portico with balcony above, the elaborate tracery, and the crenellations on the rooflines. Constructed of local red brick, white Bedford limestone is used for accent. A wide segmental arch with moulding frames the covered entry; the doors are placed to the right and left, in the base of the towers. Above the arch there are spandrels filled with floral relief ornament. The piers to either side of the arch conclude with tall pointed finials.

The north wall above the balcony has three large segmental arched windows with stone surrounds. Shallow stepped buttresses in brick with triangular capstones separate the windows. The honeycomb window tracery is applied to the windows rather than the structure. A date stone, 1913, is located above the window.

To the east, the tower is three stories in height with the third level having tracery windows and no glazing. The western tower is two stories in height. At the corners of the towers are diagonal buttresses with triangular capstones. Narrow slit windows are irregularly placed on the towers and the eastern tower also has a round window which is solid, not glazed, and has a stone tracery pattern. Bands of stone stringcourses are on the façade and those on the towers have dentils. Using structural and decorative features from various historical eras, the style of St. Paul's is Georgian.

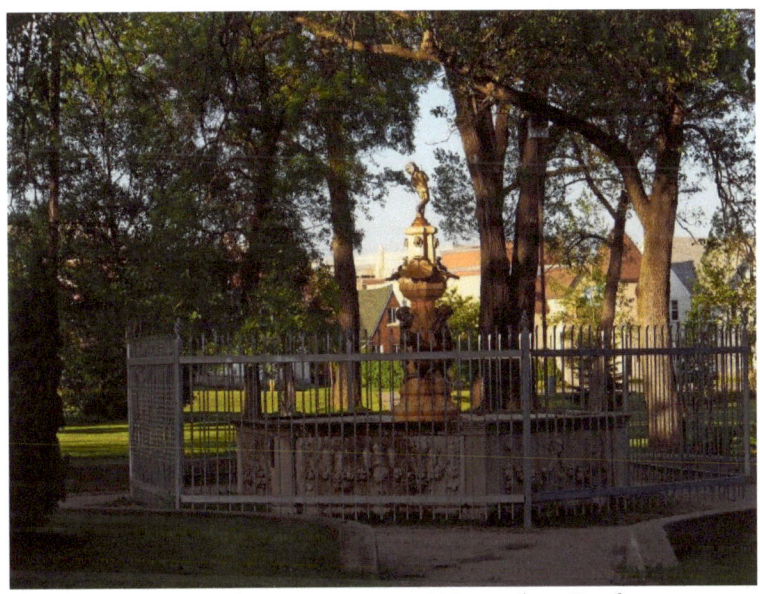

Hogarth Fountain in Waverley Park

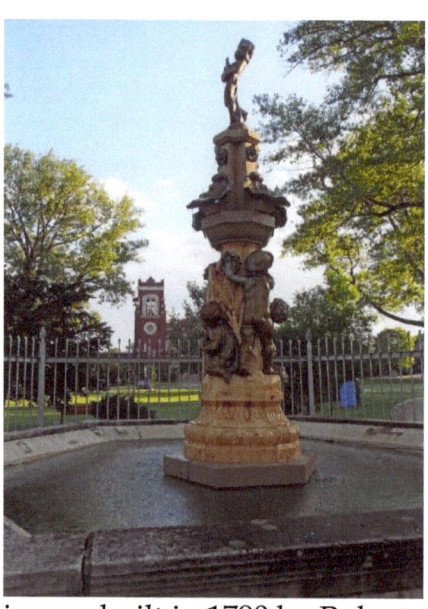

Hogarth Fountain was built in 1790 by Robert Adam in the Renaissance style. It forms the centrepiece of Waverley Park.

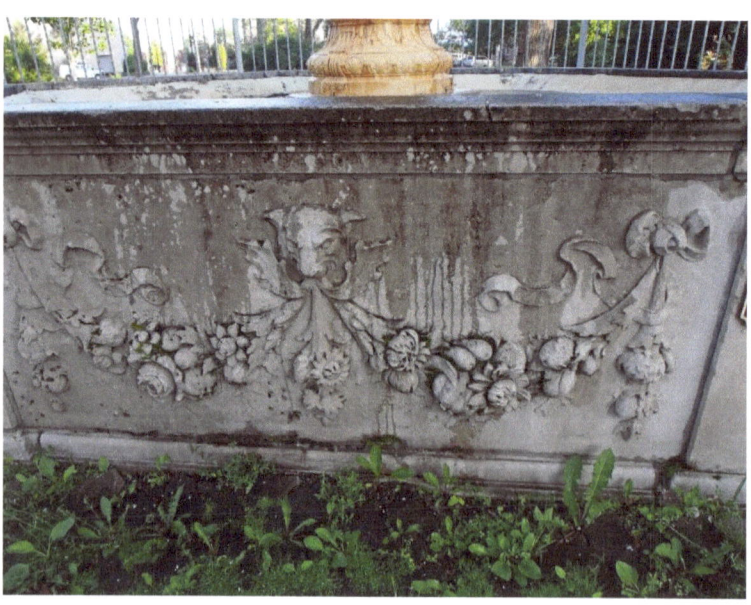

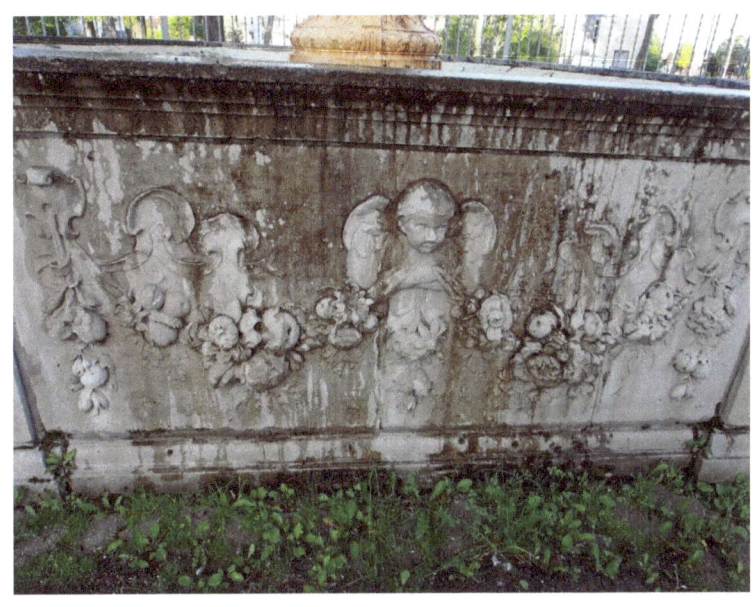

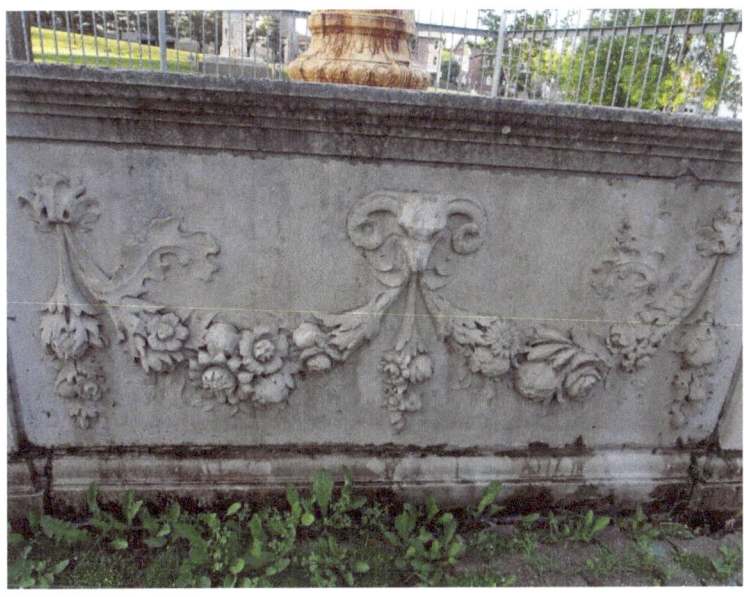

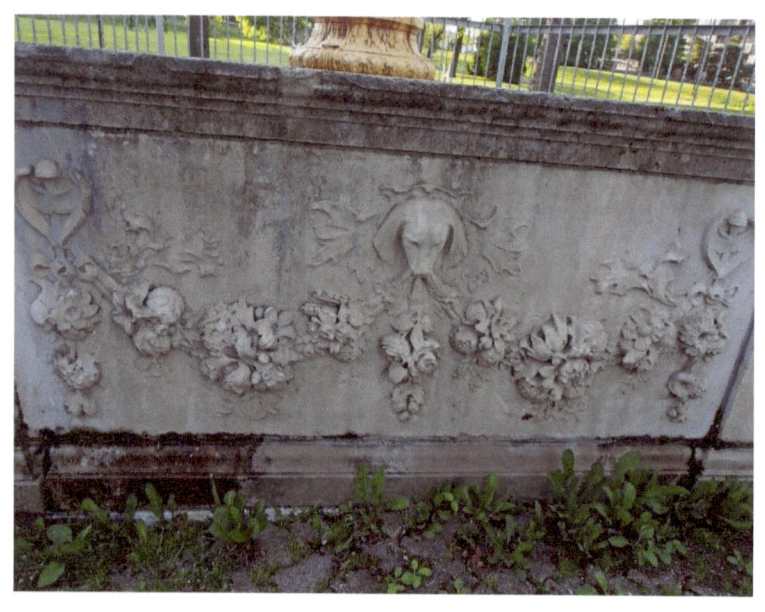

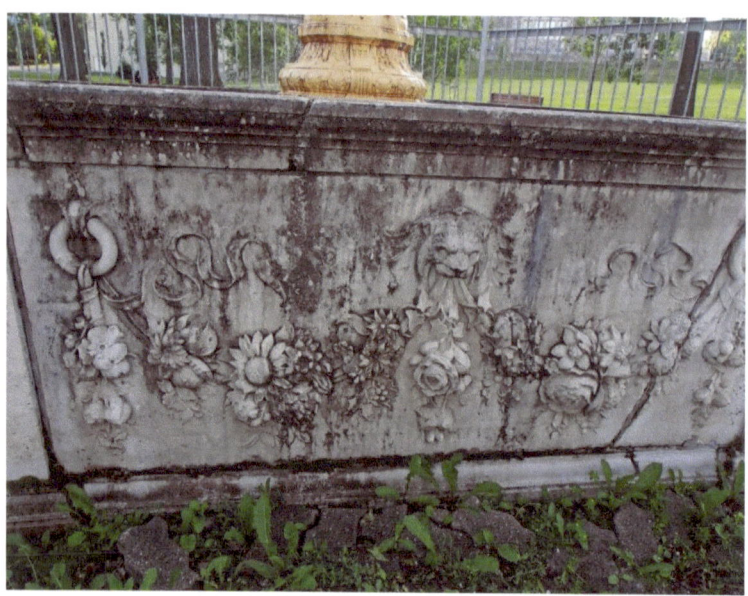

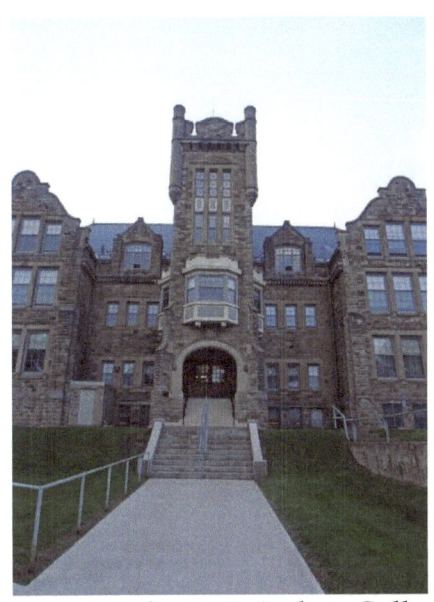

401 Red River Road – Port Arthur Collegiate Institute was constructed in 1909 of Simpson Island stone in the Queen Anne style. Due to decreasing enrollment, the school was closed in 2007. Lakehead University purchased the building and it is now the Bora Laskin Faculty of Law.

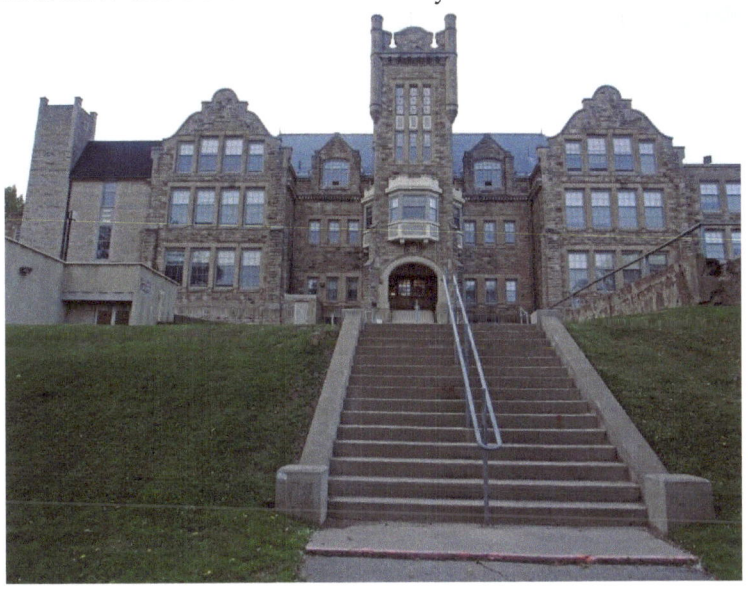

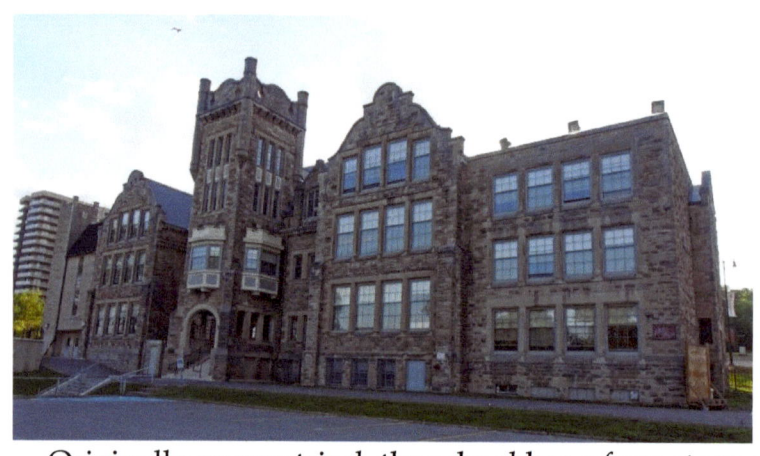

Originally symmetrical, the school has a four-storey central tower flanked by two three-storey wings. The curved step-gables of the wings repeat the curved crenellations atop the tower. Rounded battlements project from the topmost corners of the tower and oriel windows from the second level. The entrance is on the first floor of the tower and reached through a round arch. Both the tower and the wings have buttresses at the corners.

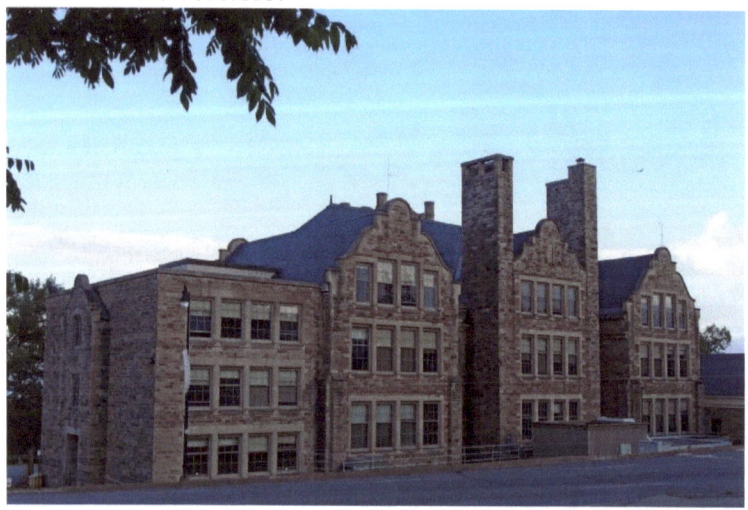

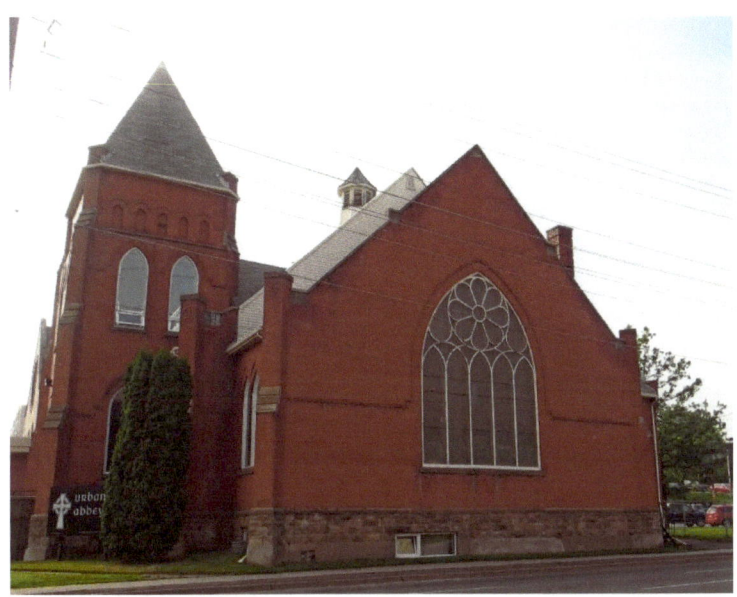

308 Red River Road – First Baptist Church - now Urban Abbey – Built in 1908 in the Late Gothic Revival style with pointed-arched windows, steeply sloping gables, and buttresses along the corners. Simpson Island (Nipigon) stone is used for the foundation and the caps for buttresses, with brick used for the remainder. There is a large arched window facing Algoma Street, composed of a rosette and five lancets.

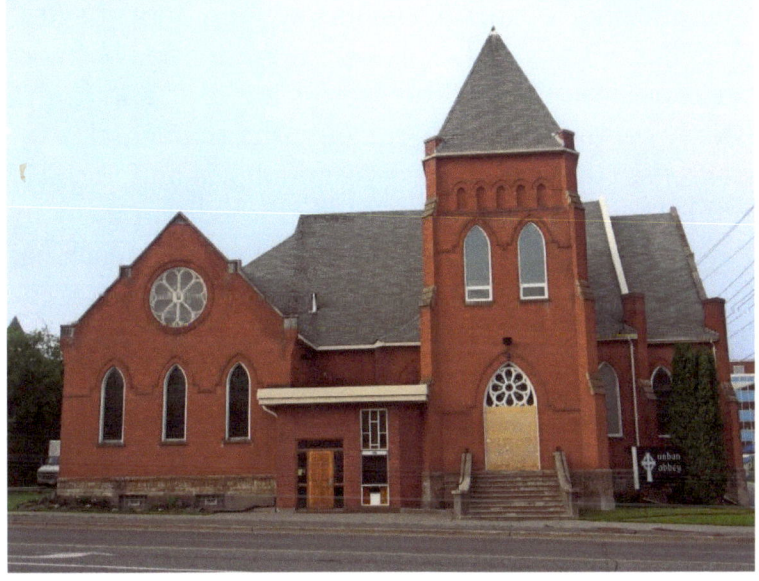

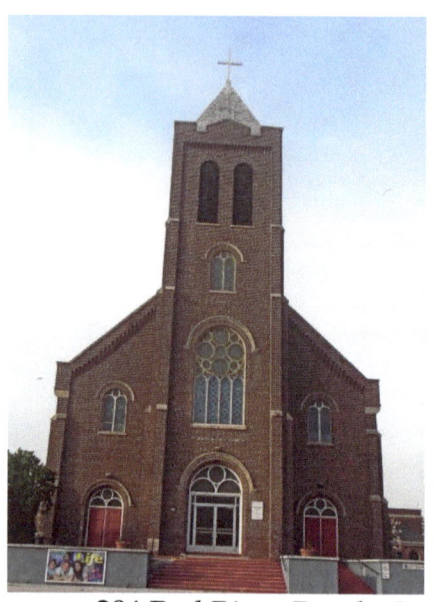 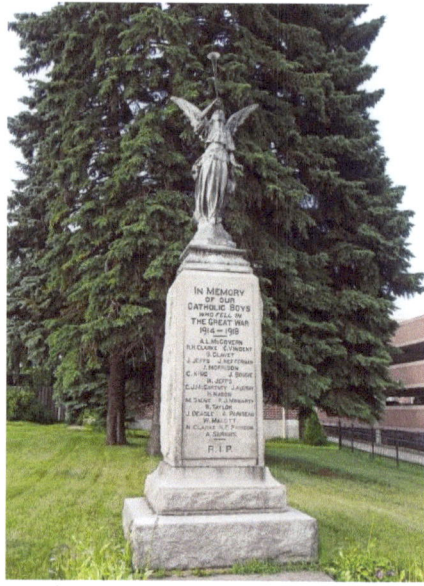

294 Red River Road - St. Andrew's Roman Catholic Church, A.D. 1924, is traditional with its longitudinal plan and Romanesque style details. The windows and doors have round arches with stone label surrounds. Stepped buttresses in pairs project from the corners of the building and from the four-storey central projecting tower with ornamental crenellations. The tower has a pyramidal roof and rises 117 feet and is topped with a cross. Along the sides of the church, there are buttresses with a large window between each pair. The large window above the main entrance in the tower is elaborated with many circles above the four rounded-arch windows included within the same framework. The stain glass repeats the circular motif with crosses.

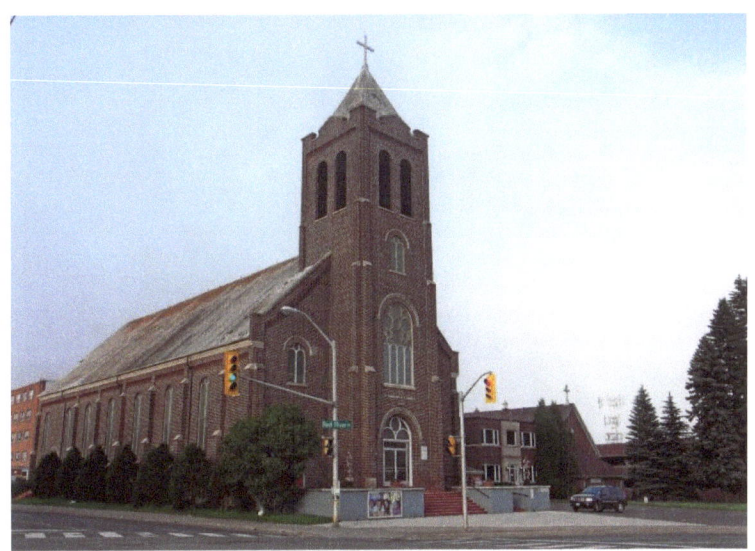

294 Red River Road

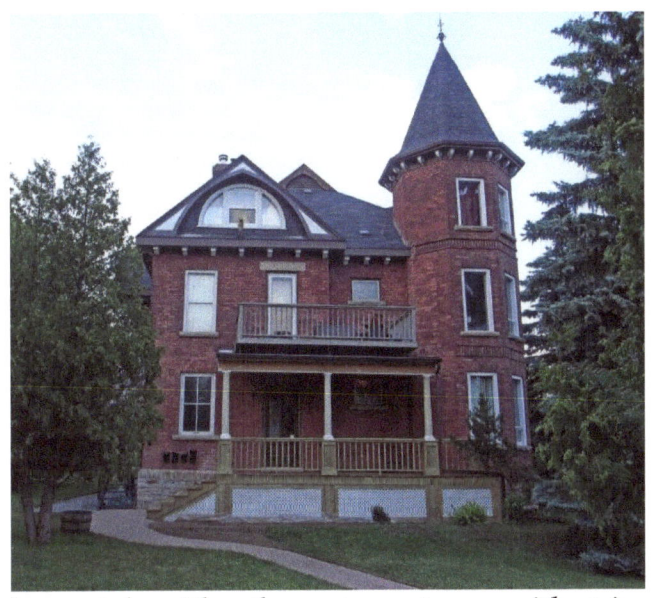

Queen Anne style with a three-storey tower with string courses between the windows; there are cornice brackets below the octagonal roof, and along the rest of the roofline; there is a second floor balcony above the veranda.

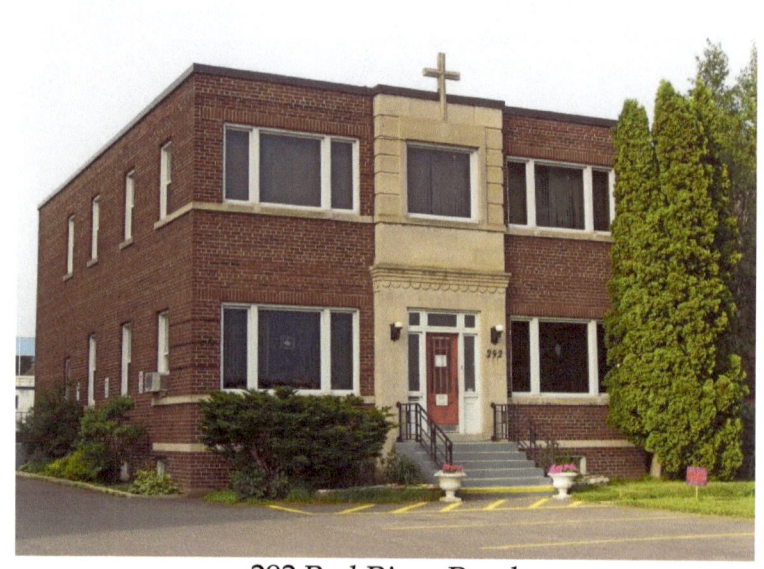

292 Red River Road

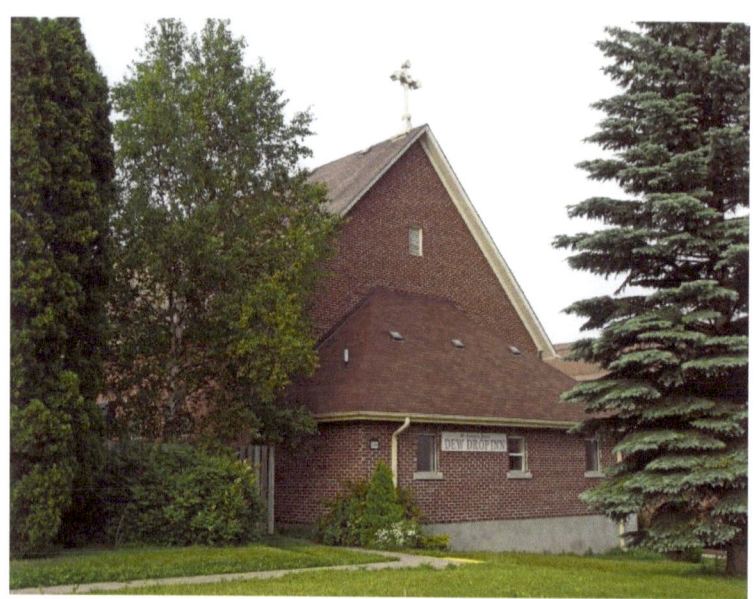

286 Red River Road – St. Andrew's Parish Dew Drop Inn

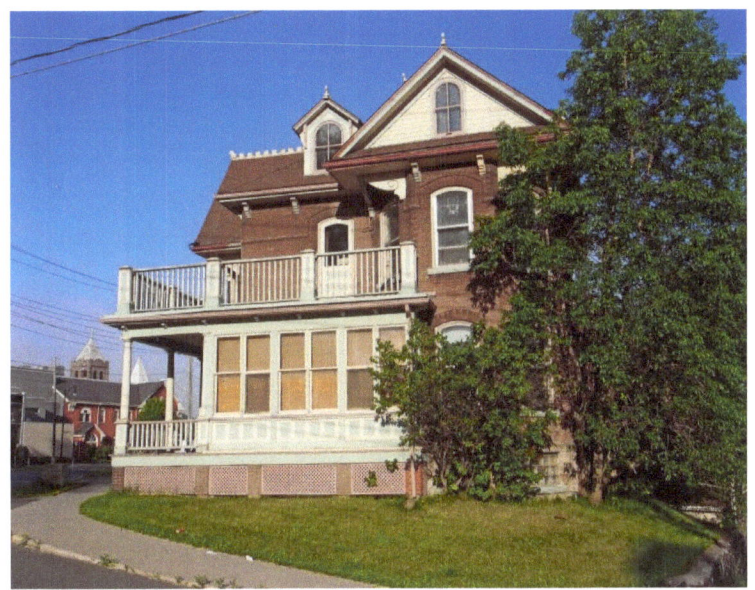

Dormer, fretwork, cornice brackets, wraparound balcony on second floor, partially enclosed wraparound veranda on ground level

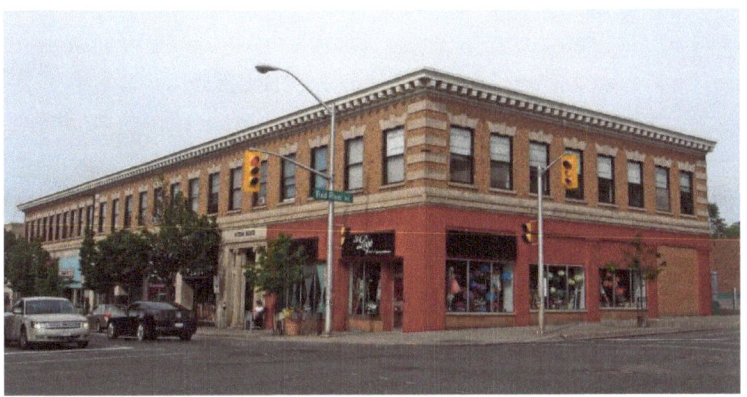

Red River Road and Court Street South – Ruttan Block with Ionic capitals on the pillars surrounding the entrance; cornice brackets under the roofline, rectangular windows with prominent dichromatic keystones, string course separating the two floors

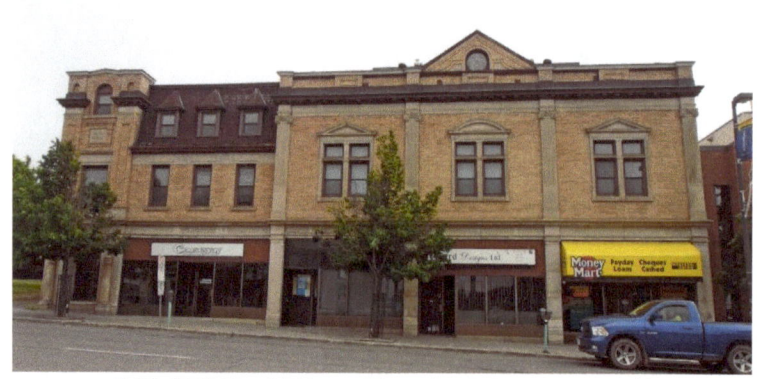

262-270 Red River Road – Masonic Hall

Known as Shuniah Lodge, this stone, brick and concrete building was built in 1910 to replace the old Masonic temple that was destroyed by fire in 1909. The first floor is made of cut stone, and the entrance features carved marble pilasters and decorative panels. Originally there was a dome on the roof over the entrance. The central portion of the building has a Mansard roof of French design. The building's windows are decorated with alternating round and triangular pediments above them. Commercial space occupies the ground floor, while the lodge is located above.

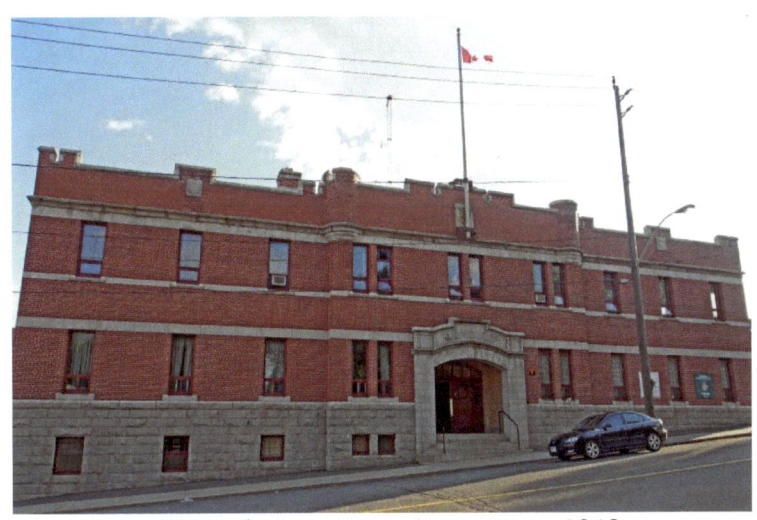

317 Park Avenue – Armoury - 1913

This two-storey building, constructed of red brick with cut stone detailing, reflects the influence of the Beaux-Arts style using medieval military motifs. There is a crenellated parapet on the façade and rear of the building. There are rounded battlements on the corners of the projecting central bay and the word "Armoury" carved in relief above the main entrance. Brick pilasters along the side of the building divide it into 13 bays and large semi-circular windows are along each side. The continuous stone lintels and window wells form a stark contrast with the red brick and the walls. The overall effect of the building is one of strength and solidity, which suits its military purpose.

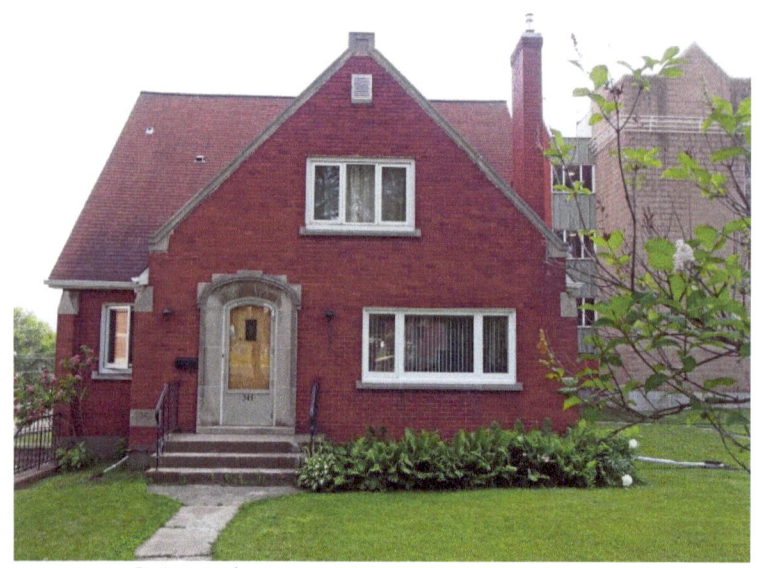
345 Park Avenue - 1956 – steep gable

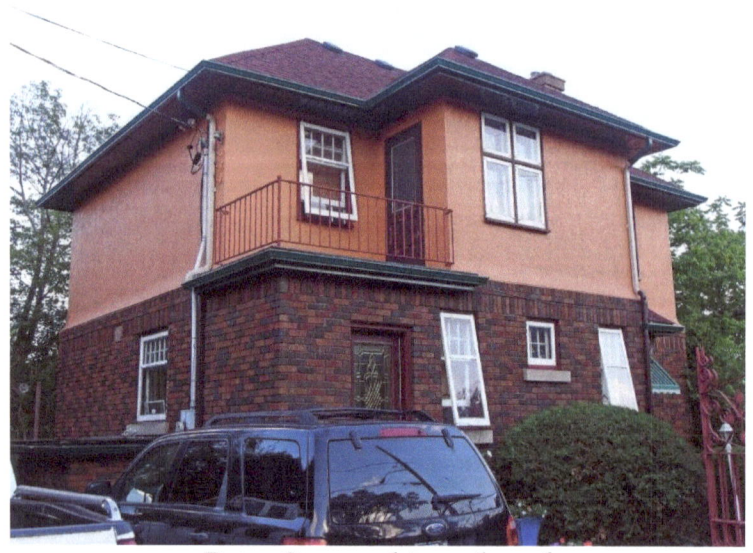
Peter Street – hipped roof

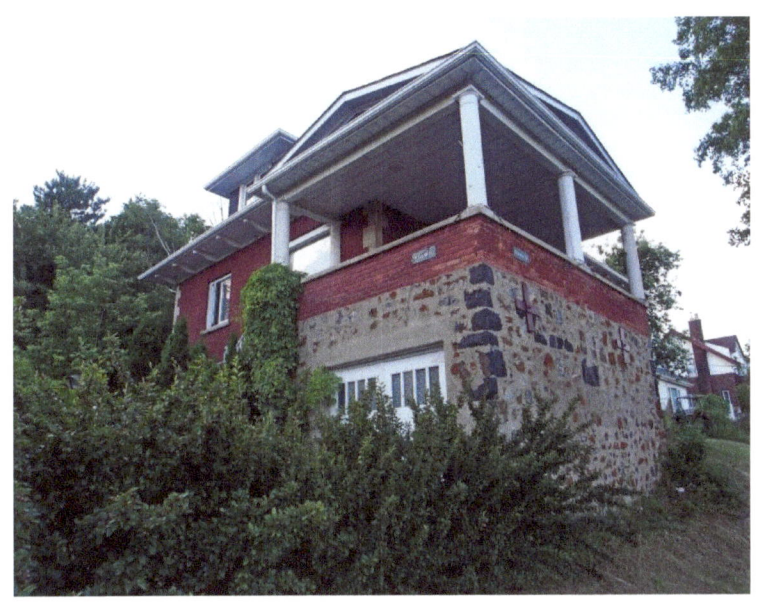

2 Peter Street – stone foundation, corner quoins, dormer in attic, pediments above porch

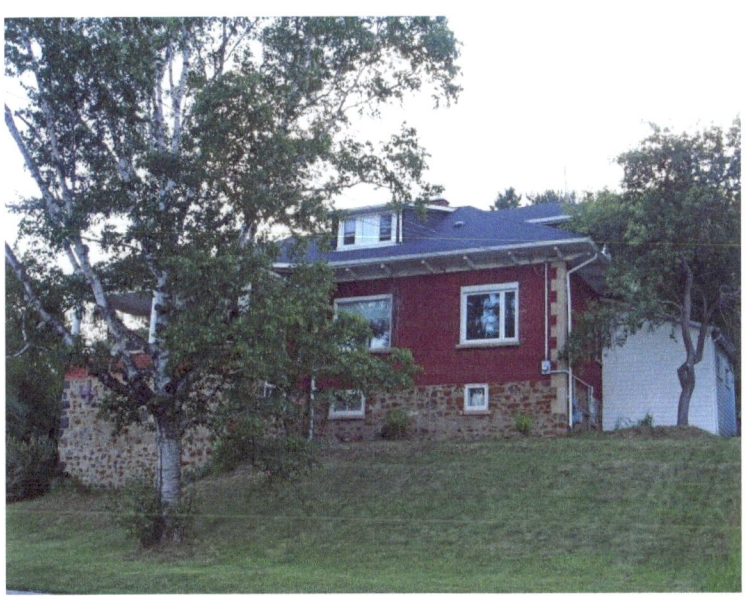

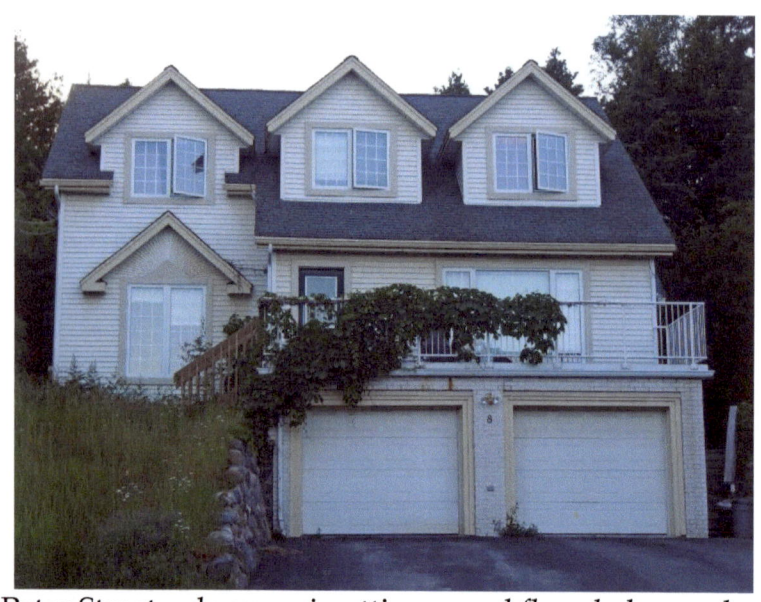

8 Peter Street – dormers in attic, second floor balcony above double garage

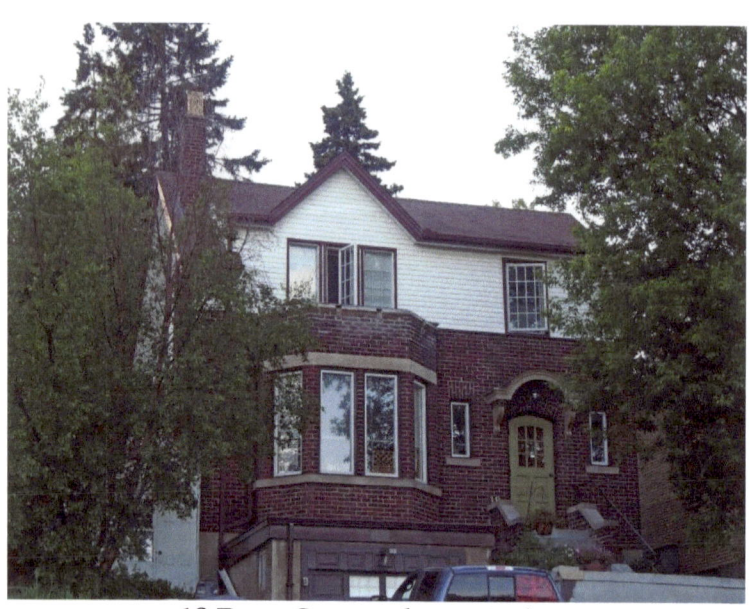

18 Peter Street – bay window

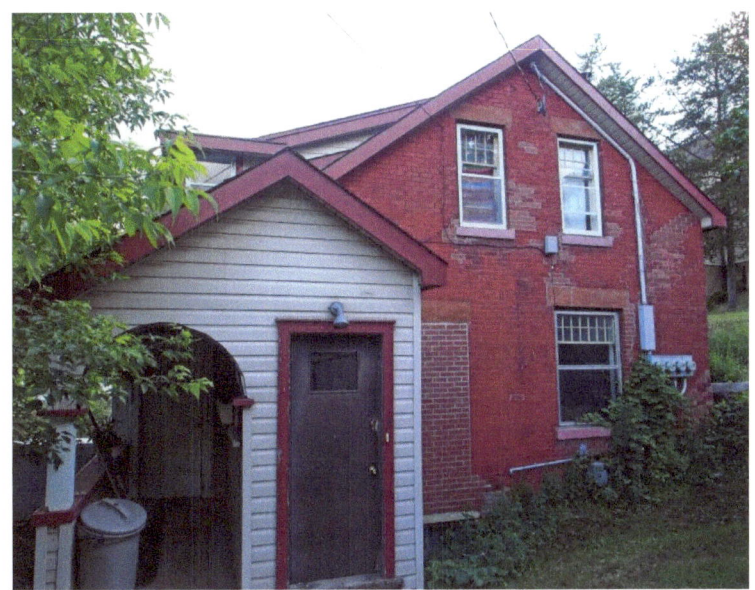

Hebert Street

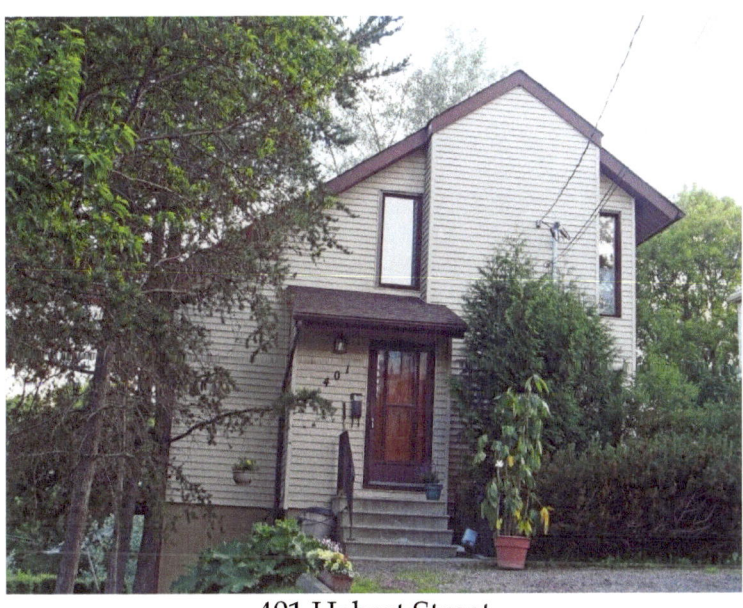

401 Hebert Street

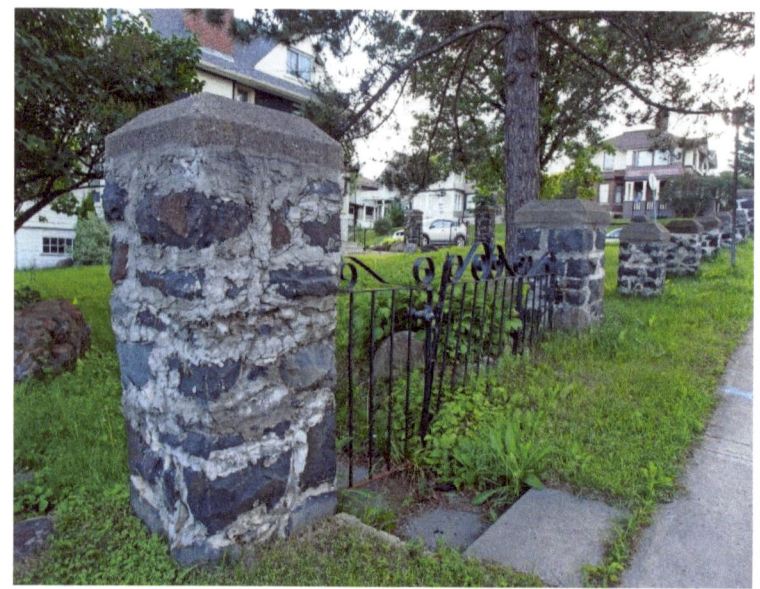
Pillars and wrought iron fence along Hebert Street

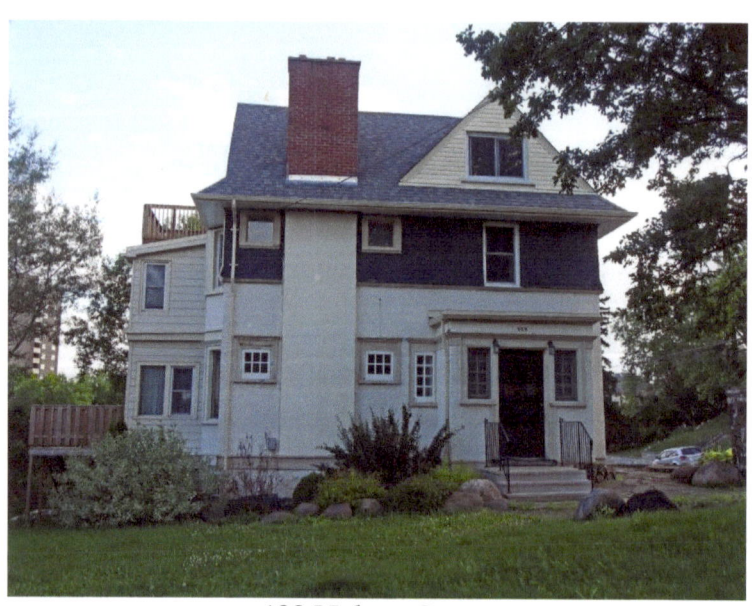
409 Hebert Street

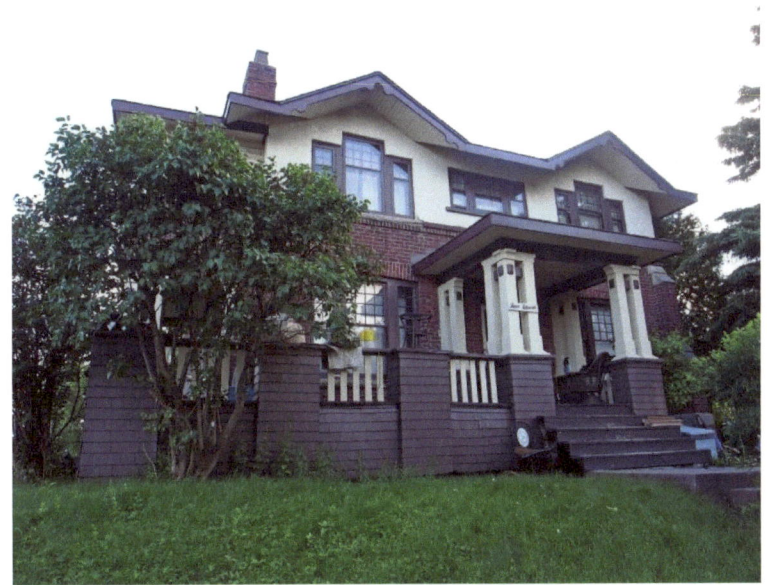

411 College Street – triple-Palladian-like windows in second floor facade

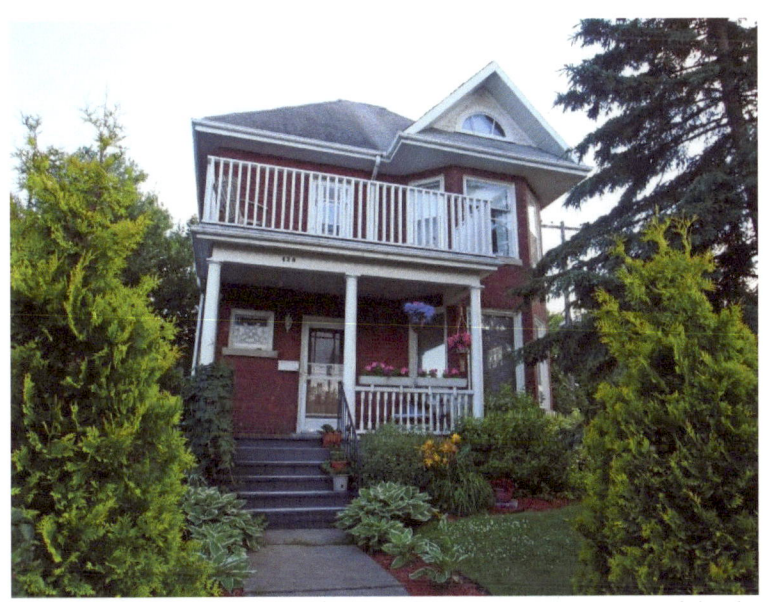

429 College Street – hipped roof, 2½-storey tower-like bay topped with a gable with a semi-circular window, second floor balcony

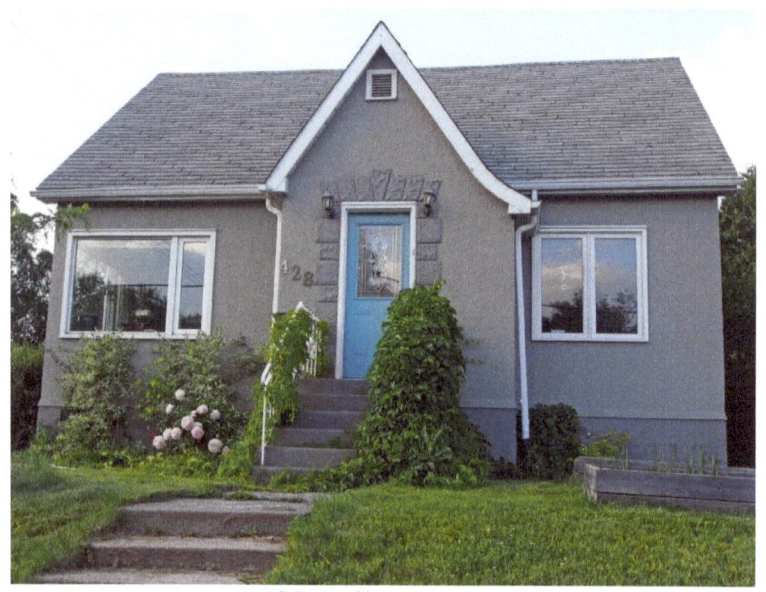

428 College Street

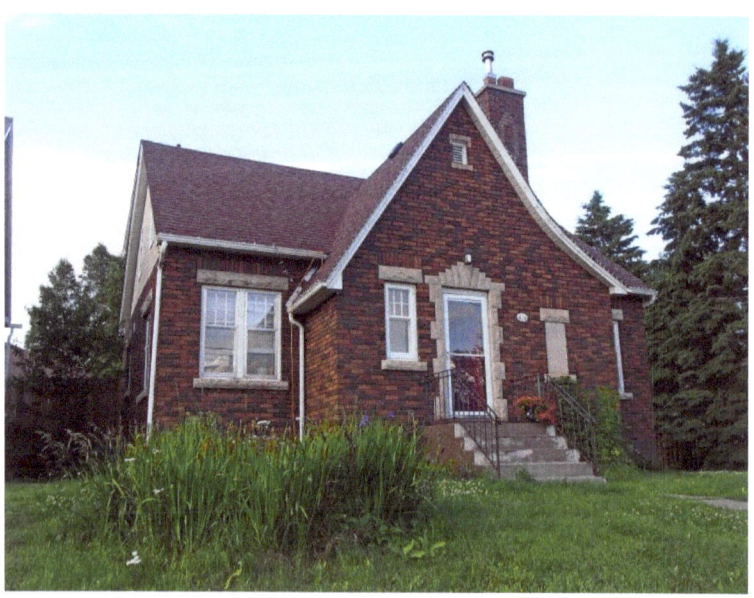

424 College Street – Arts and Crafts style

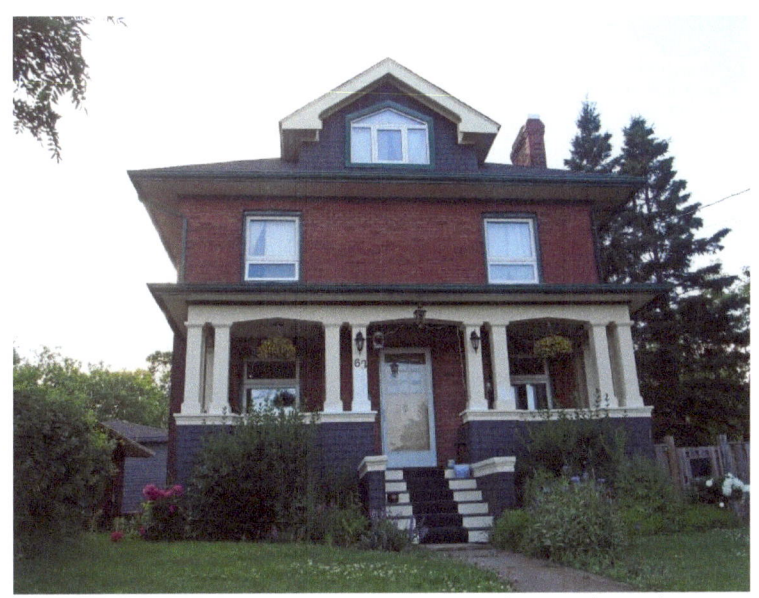

62 College Street – dormer in hipped roof

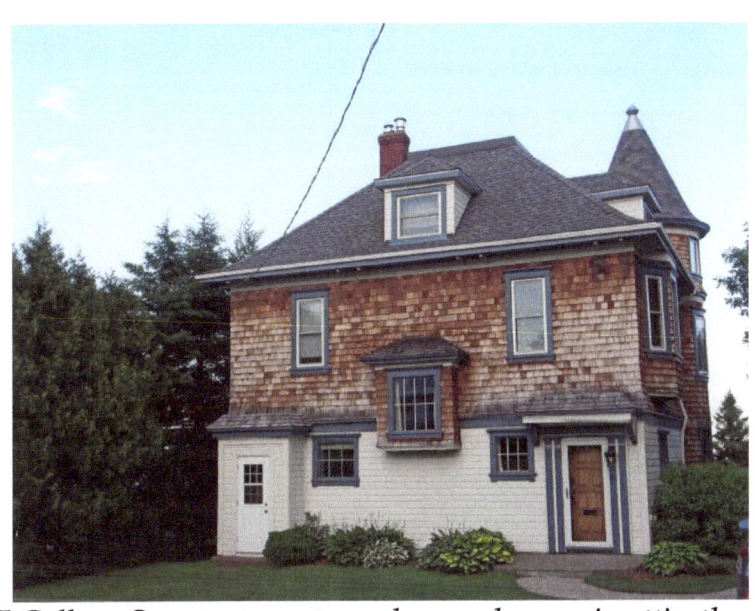

65 College Street – two-storey home, dormer in attic, three-storey tower with conical roof

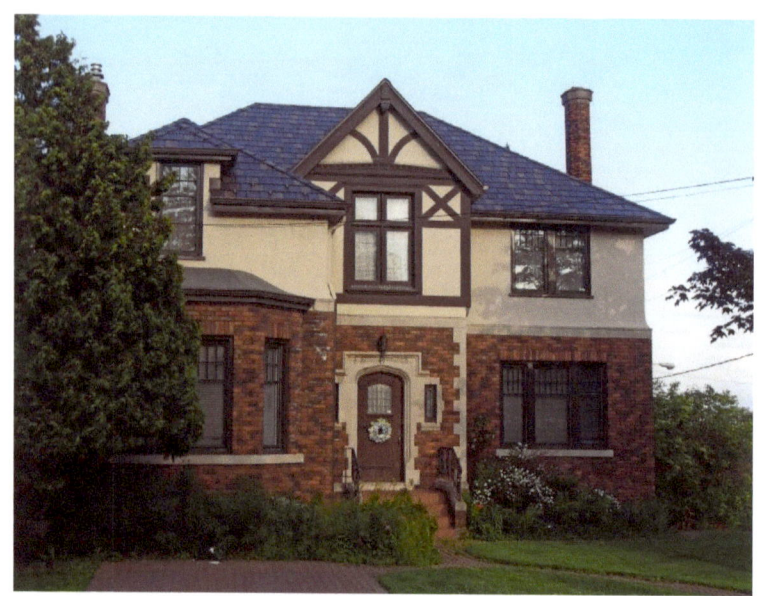

49 College Street – Arts and Crafts style with Tudor half-timbering on gable of two-storey frontispiece, bay window

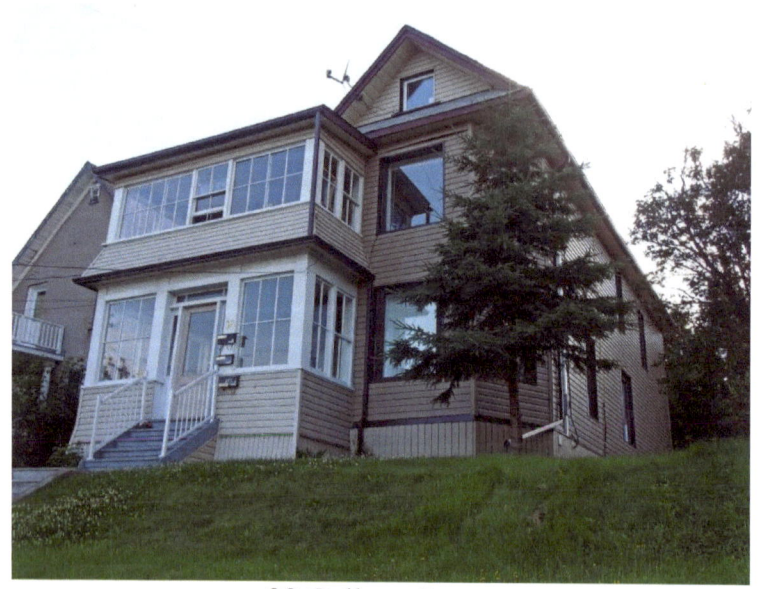

38 College Street

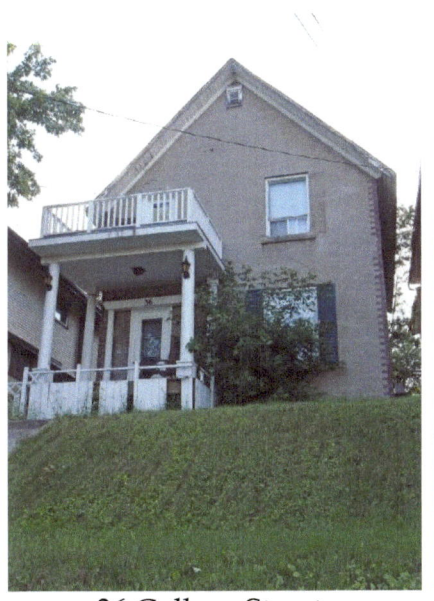

36 College Street
Gothic

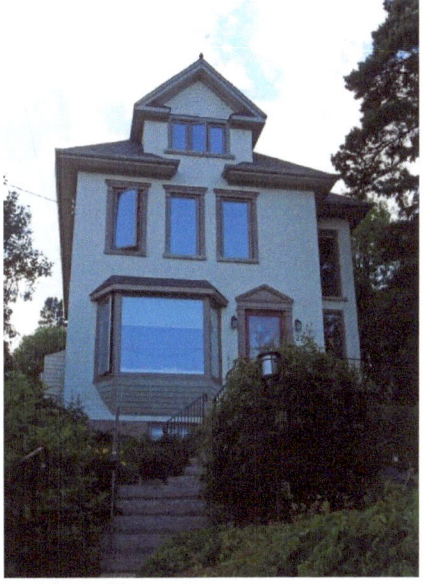

22 College Street
dormer in hipped roof

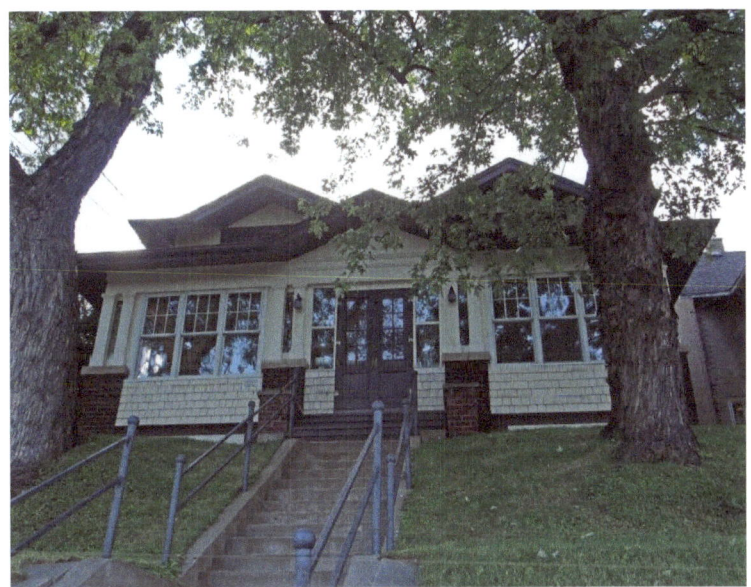

College Street

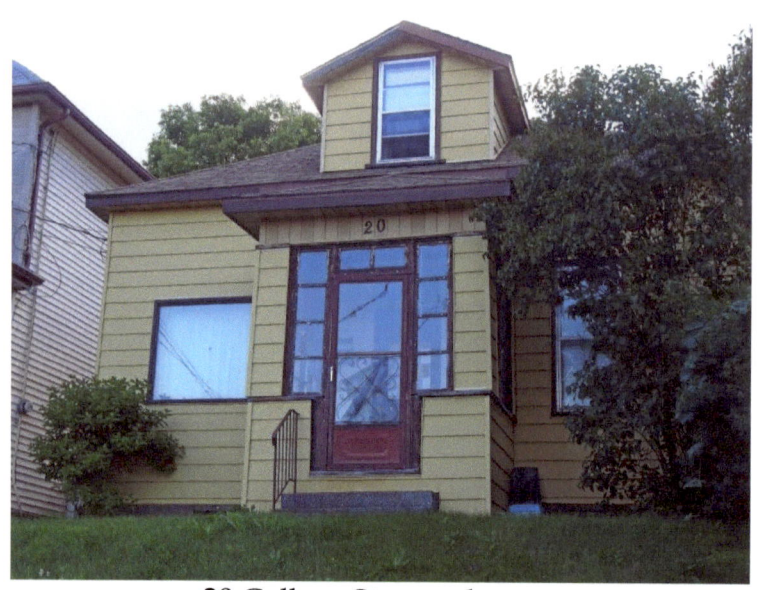
20 College Street - dormer

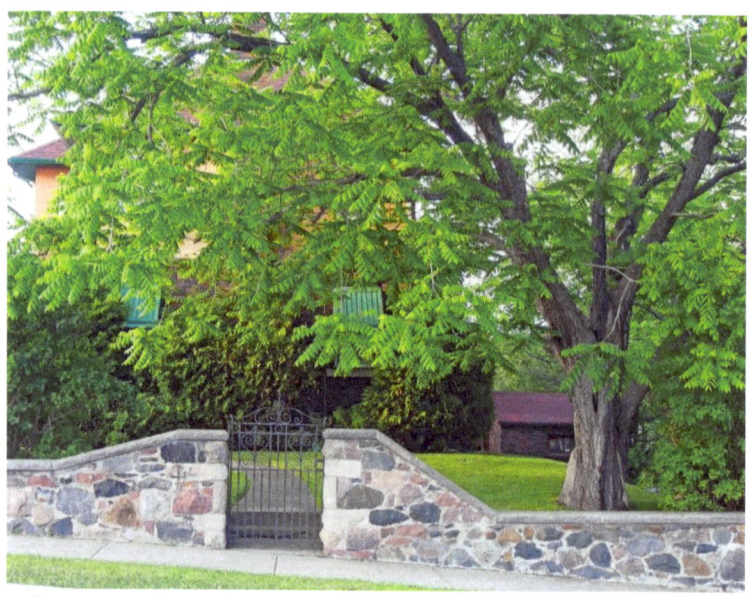
Stone wall and wrought iron gate on College Street

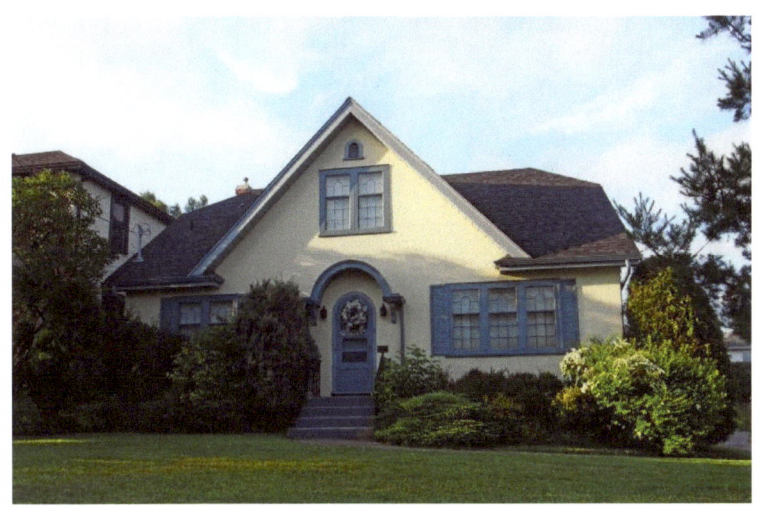

Dufferin Street

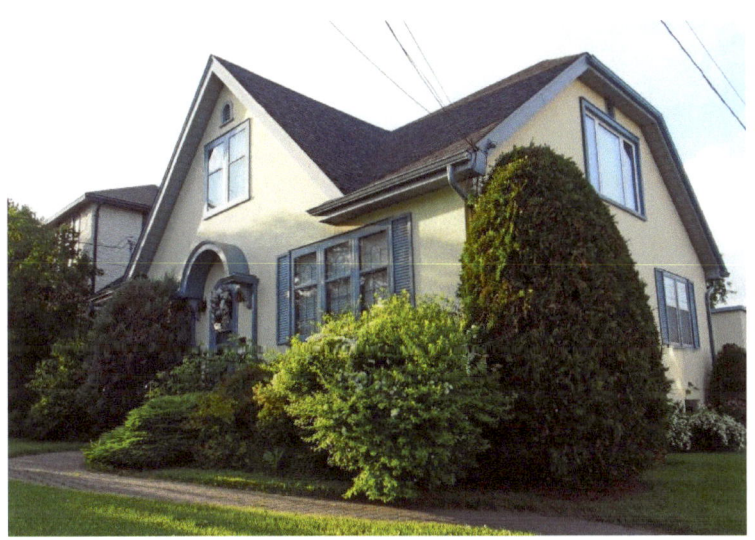

Chipped gable on end

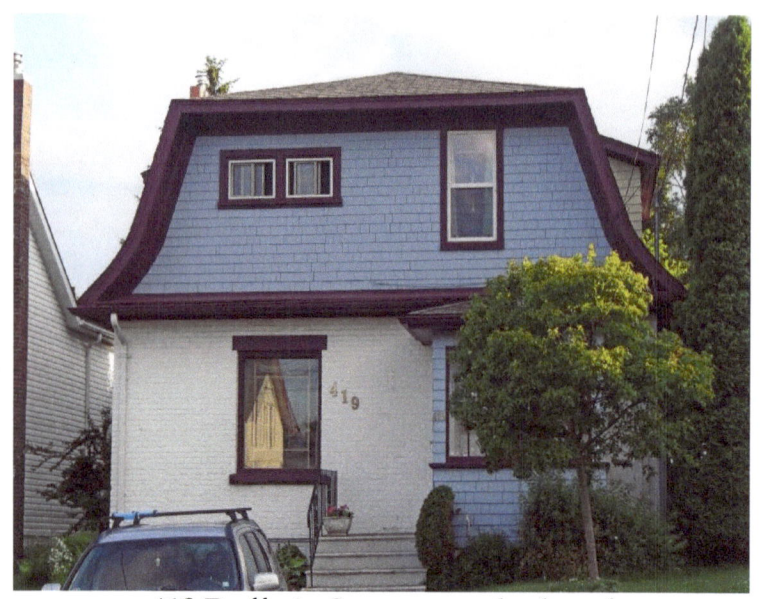

419 Dufferin Street – gambrel roof

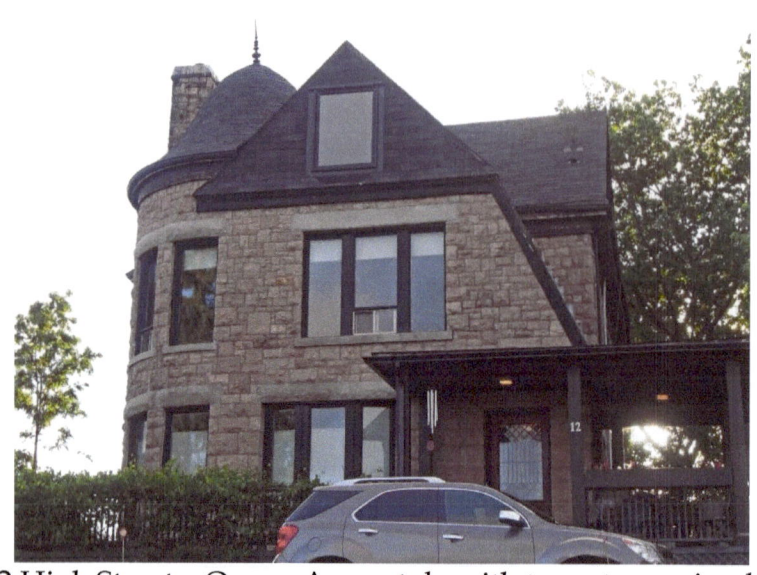

12 High Street – Queen Anne style with two-storey circular tower with dome roof

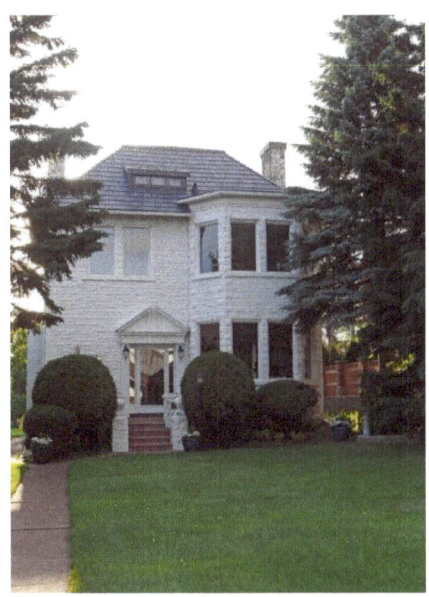

High Street – hipped roof with small shed dormer; two-storey bay window, broken pediment above entrance, sidelights

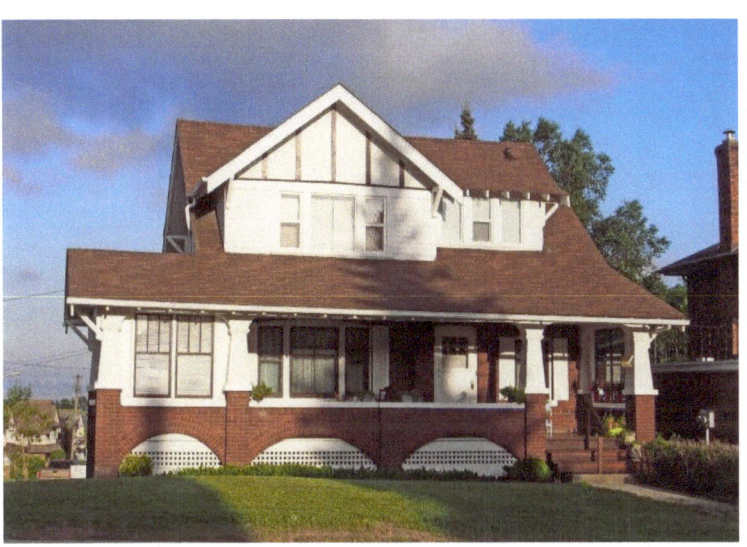

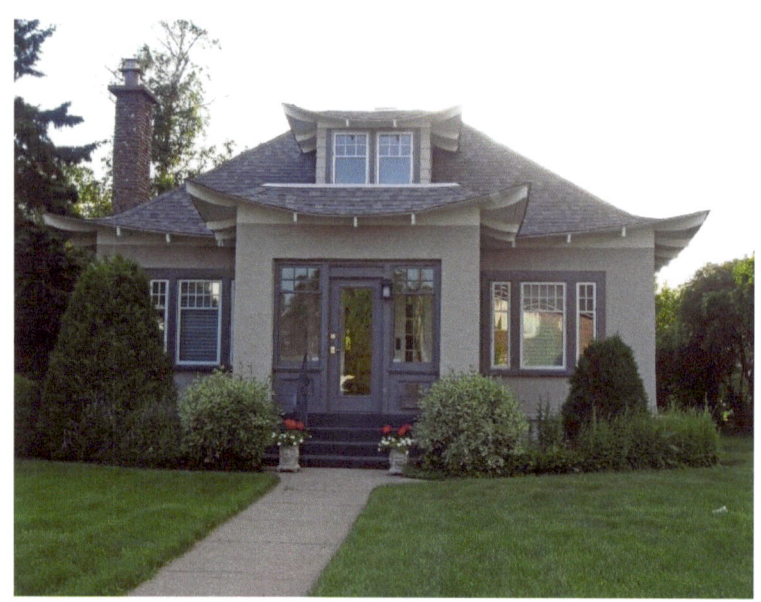

30 High Street

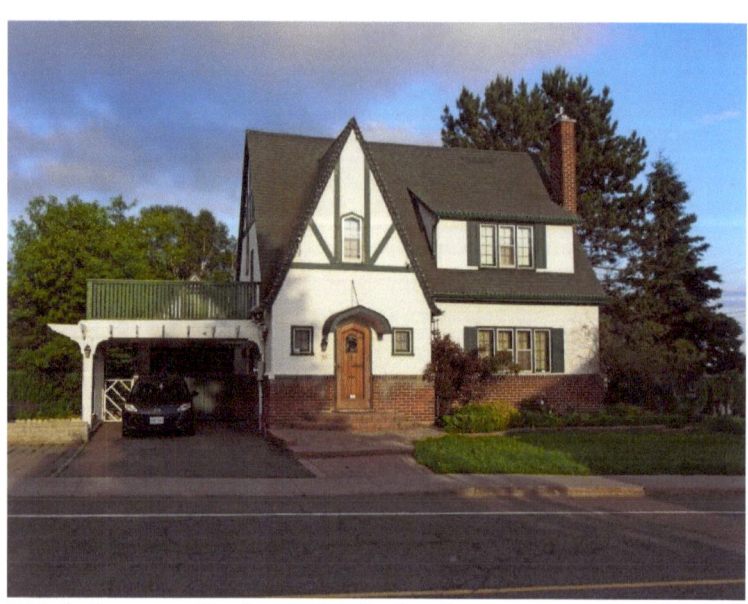

35 High Street – Tudor half-timbering on steep gables, shed dormer in attic

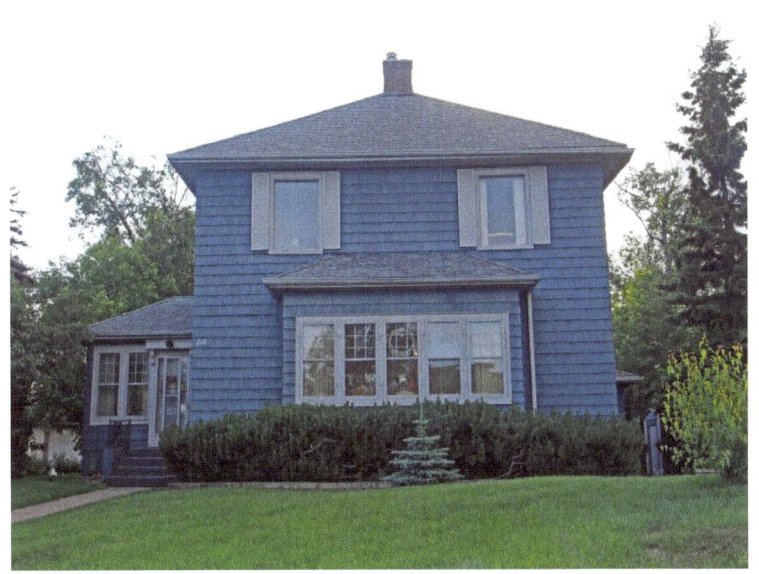

36 High Street – hipped roof

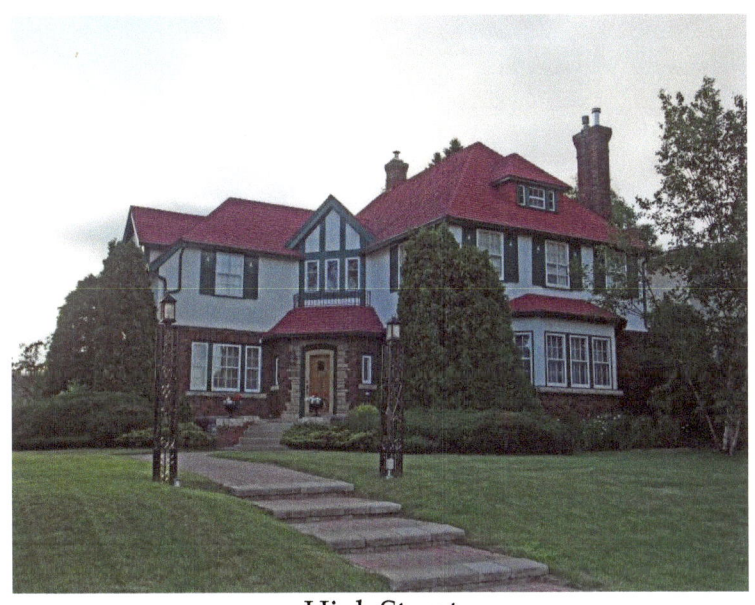

High Street

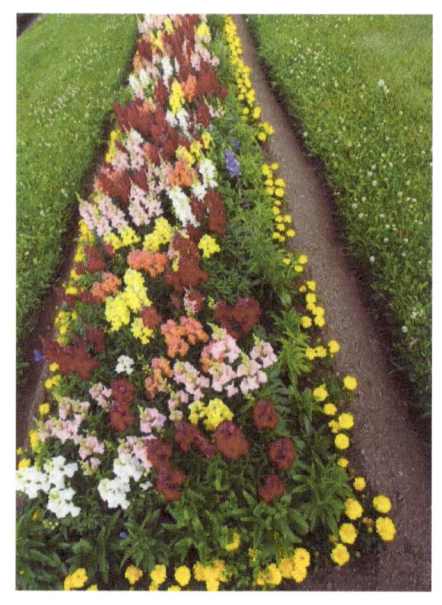

Gardens on High Street

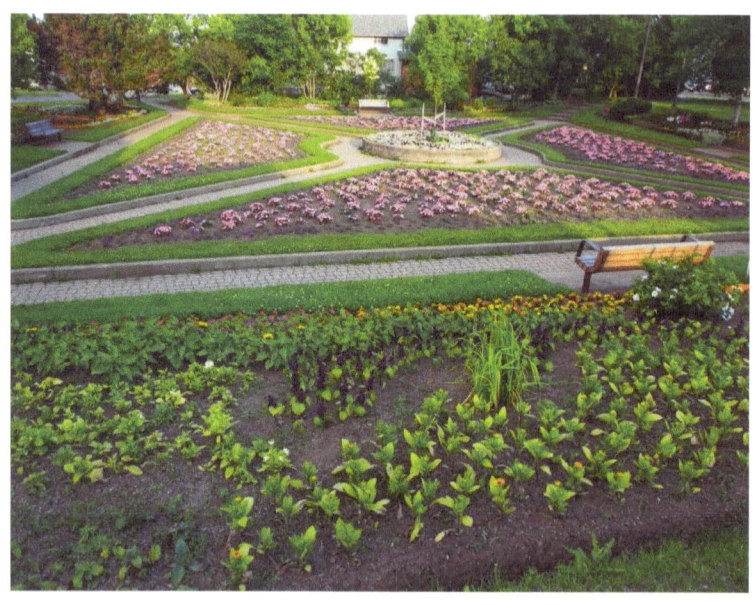

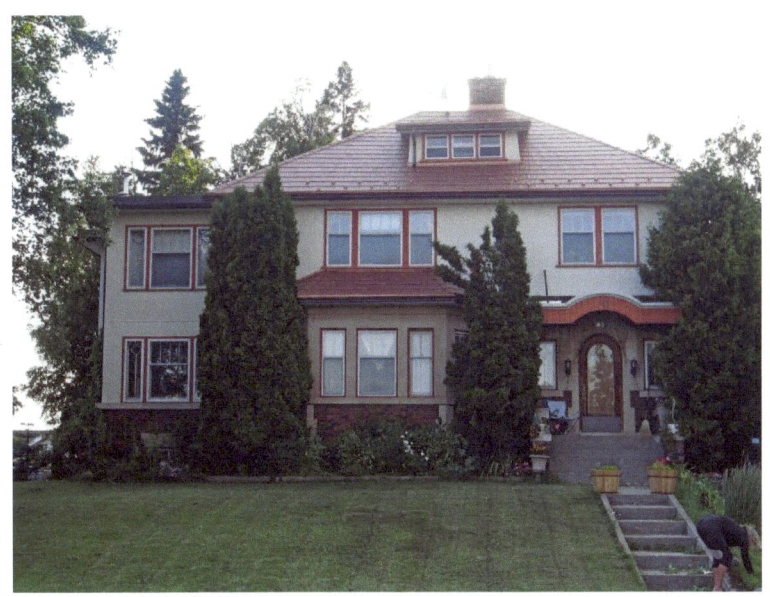
40 High Street – hipped roof with dormer

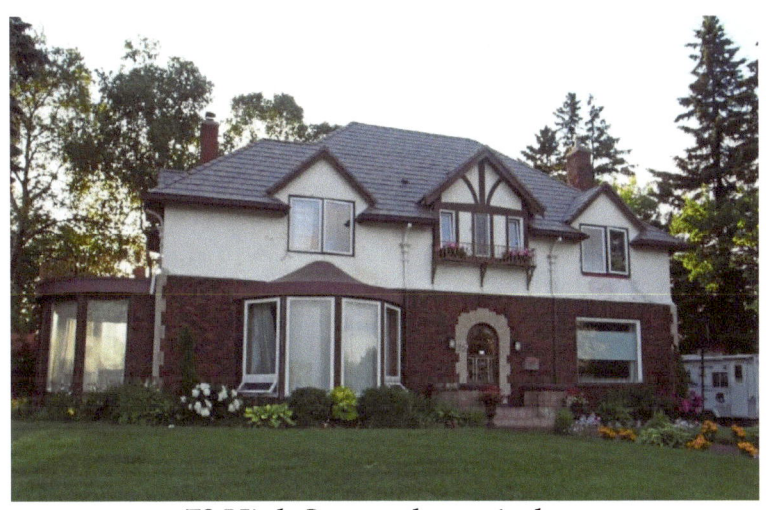
70 High Street – bay window

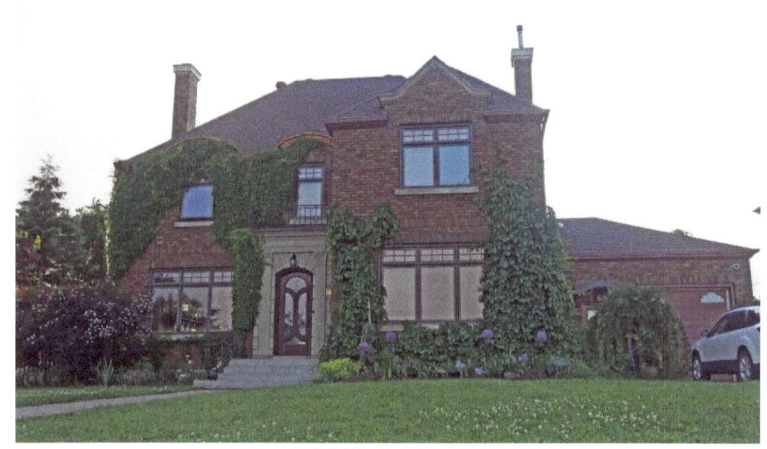

84 High Street

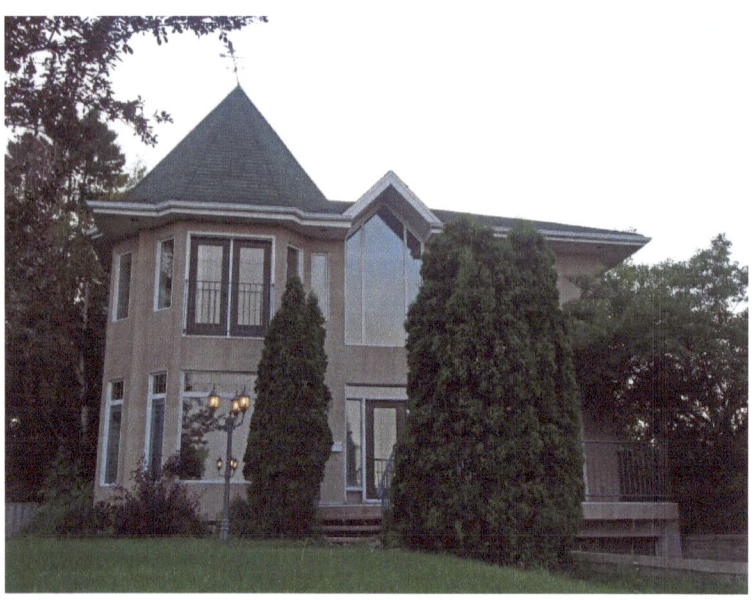

High Street

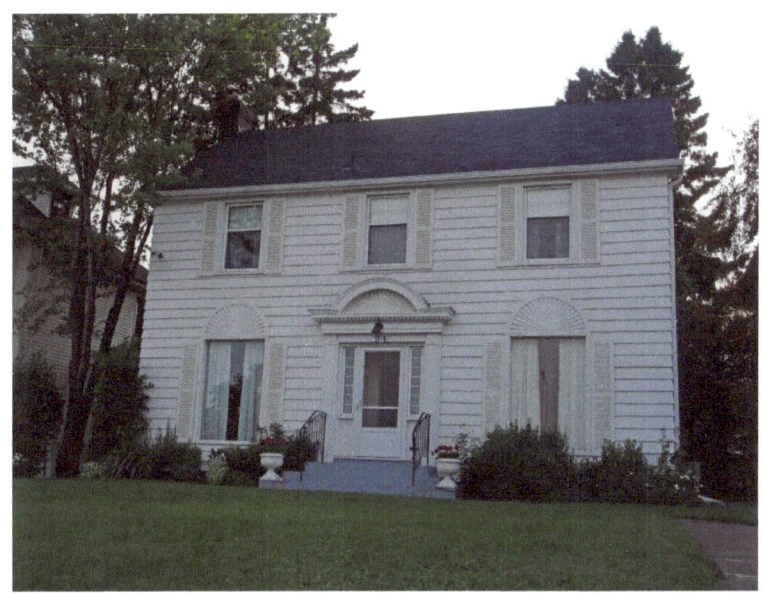

94 High Street - Georgian

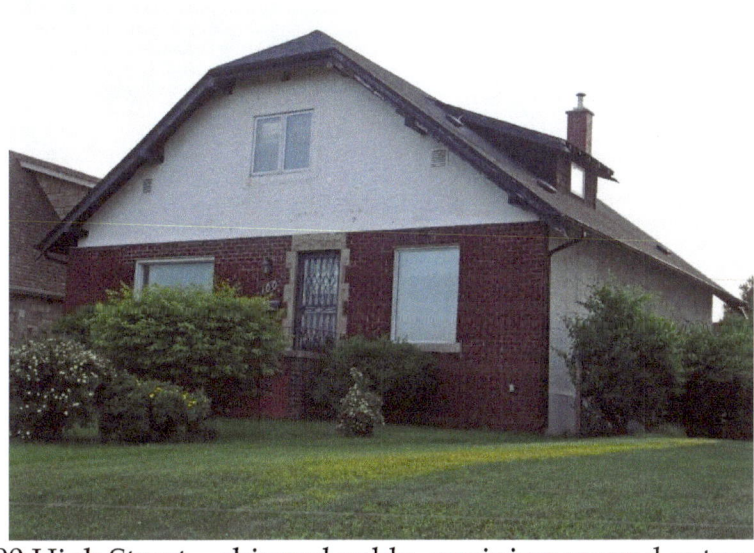

100 High Street – chipped gable, quoining around entrance

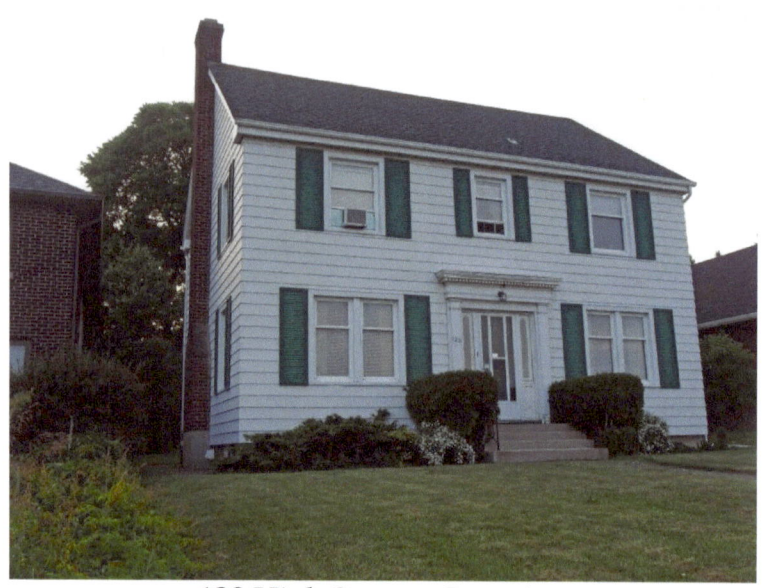

120 High Street - Georgian

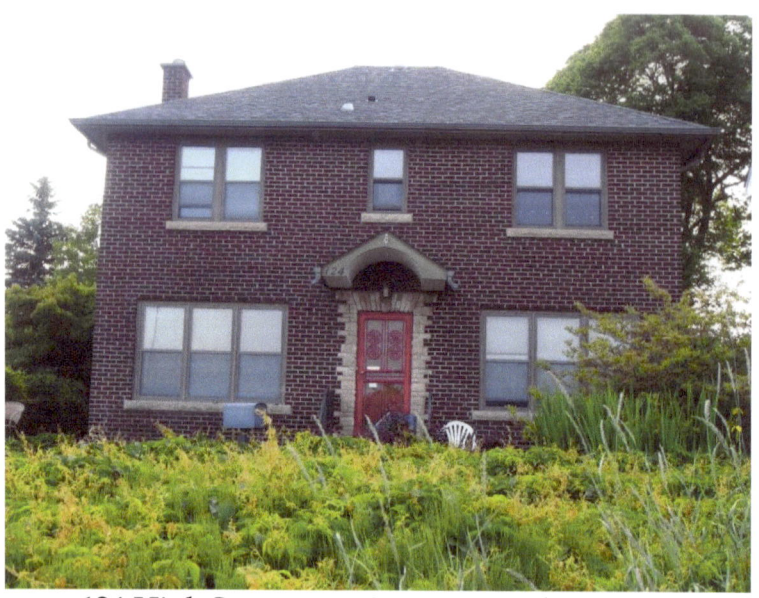

124 High Street - quoining around entrance

Architectural Terms

Battlement: A design for a parapet that has alternating solid parts and openings, originally used for defense, but later used as a decorative motif. Example: 401 Red River Road, Page 18	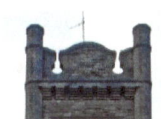
Bay Window: A window that projects out from a wall, in a semicircular, rectangular, or polygonal design. Used frequently in Gothic and Victorian designs. Example: 18 Peter Street, Page 28	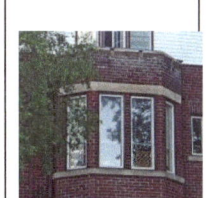
Brackets: a decorative or weight-bearing structural element which forms a right angle with one side against a wall and the other under a projecting surface such as an eave or roof. Example: 10 Algoma Street South, Page 10	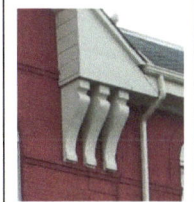
Buttress: a masonry structure built against or projecting from a wall which serves to support or reinforce the wall. In Canadian architecture, they are sometimes used for decoration. Example: 349 Waverley Street, Page 12	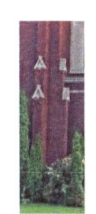
Stone architecture: Refers to the use of stones embedded in mortar as a method for erecting walls on houses and commercial buildings. Example: 2 Peter Street, Page 27	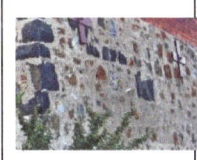

Course: continuous horizontal row or layer of stone or brick. Example: Red River Road, Page 21	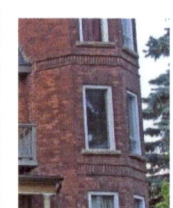
Crenellation: a series of depressed openings, like a battlement, but with more space between the openings. A crenelle (or kernel) in medieval times was an opening in a battlement, a loophole through which arrows and missiles could be launched. Example: 349 Waverley Street, Page 12	
Cupola: A domed or curved roof rising from a building as a decorative element. Example: 30 Algoma Street South, Page 9	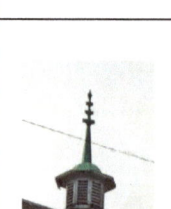
Dentil Moulding: an even series of rectangles used as ornamental decoration in cornices. Example: 349 Waverley Street, Page 12	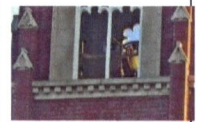
Dichromatic brickwork: the use of two colours of brick, tile or slate to decorate a façade. Example: Red River Road and Court Street South, Page 23	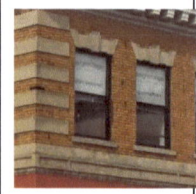

Dormer: (French for "sleep") a gable end window that pierces through the plane of a sloping roof surface to create usable space in the top floor or attic of a building by adding headroom. Example: Waverley Street, Page 11	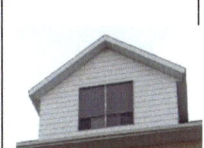
Fretwork: interlaced decorative design resembling a bracket Example: Red River Road, Page 23	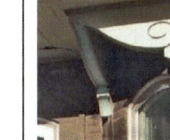
Frontispiece: a portion of the façade of a building, usually a centred doorway that is slightly raised from the rest of the building, usually has extensive ornamentation. Frontispieces are usually Classical in design with white columned porches. Example: 49 College Street, Page 34	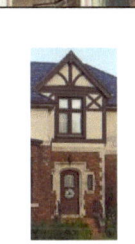
Gable: the triangular portion of a wall between the edges of a sloping roof. Example: 345 Park Avenue, Page 26	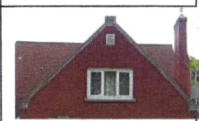
Gambrel Roof: a symmetrical two-sided roof with two slopes on each side; the upper slope is positioned at a shallow angle, while the lower slope is steep. It is similar to a mansard roof, but a gambrel has vertical gable ends instead of being hipped at the four corners of the building. Example: 419 Dufferin Street, Page 38	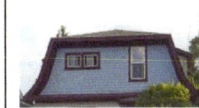

Hipped Roof: a roof where all sides slope downwards to the walls with no gables. Example: 36 High Street, Page 41	
Lancet Window: a tall, narrow window with a pointed arch at its top. Example: 308 Red River Road, Page 19	
Oriel Window - These small areas were originally set into walls and galleries for the purpose of private prayer. Over time, any projecting window or area on an upper floor was called an oriel. Example: 401 Red River Road, Page 17	
Palladian Window: a large window that is divided into three sections with the centre section larger than the two side sections and usually arched. Example: 411 College Street, Page 31	
Parapet: low wall around the edge of a roof. Example: 317 Park Avenue, Page 25	
Pediment: a triangular section above the door or portico, usually supported by columns. The inside of the triangle is called the tympanum. Example: 262-270 Red River Road, Page 24	

Pilaster: a slightly projecting column built into or applied to the face of a wall for additional structural support. Example: 262-270 Red River Road, Page 24	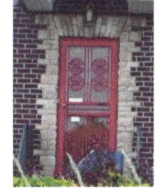
Quoin: masonry blocks at the corner of a wall, often a decorative feature, usually larger or of a different colour than the rest of the wall. Example: 124 High Street, Page 46	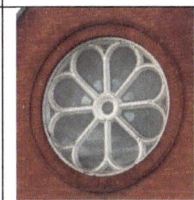
Rose Window: a circular window with ornamental tracery radiating from the centre. Example: 308 Red River Road, Page 19	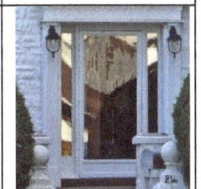
Sidelight: a vertical window that flanks a door, and is often used to emphasize the importance of a primary entrance. Example: High Street, Page 39	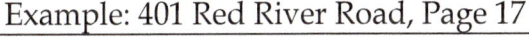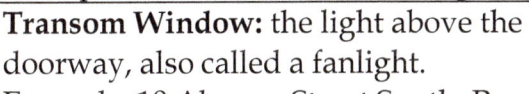
Tower: A circular, square, or octagonal vertical structure higher than the surrounding structure that is usually part of an existing building and is created either for extra defense or for a specific purpose such as a clock or a bell tower. Example: 401 Red River Road, Page 17	
Transom Window: the light above the doorway, also called a fanlight. Example: 10 Algoma Street South, Page 10	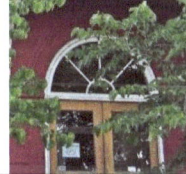

Building Styles

Arts and Crafts: The overlying theme - the house was based on the function of the house. Rooms were oriented to take advantage of the movement of the sun for warmth and light during daylight hours. Side entrances allowed for useable space on the front facade for light or garden use. Arts and Crafts houses have many of these features: wood, stone or stucco siding; low-pitched roof; wide eaves with triangular brackets; exposed roof rafters; porch with thick square or round columns; stone porch supports; exterior chimney made with stone; open floor plans with few hallways; many windows, some with stained or leaded glass; beamed ceilings; dark wood wainscoting and moldings; built-in cabinets, shelves, and seating. Example: 424 College Street, Page 32	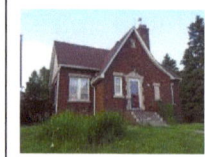
Beaux Arts: Promoters of this style sought to express the classical principles on a grand and imposing scale. Many of the Beaux Arts buildings were banks, post offices, and railway stations. The Ontario Beaux Arts style is eclectic mixing elements of Classical, Renaissance and Baroque. Often the designs have a temple-like façade, porticos with pediments, balustrades, and capitals in many styles. Example: 317 Park Avenue, Page 25	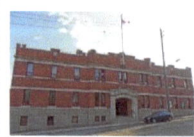

Georgian, before 1860 – This style began with the British King Georges in the 18th century. These buildings have balanced facades around a central door, medium-pitched gable roofs, and small paned windows. Example: 120 High Street, Page 46	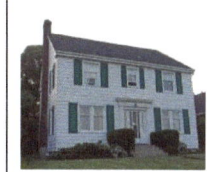
Gothic Revival, 1830-1890 – These decorative buildings have sharply-pitched gables with highly detailed verge boards, pointed-arch window openings, and dichromatic brickwork. It is a common style in Ontario. Example: 308 Red River Road, Page 19	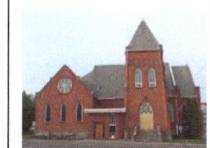
Queen Anne, 1885-1900 – This style is distinguished by an irregular outline featuring a combination of an offset tower, broad gables, projecting two-storey bays, verandahs, multi-sloped roofs, and tall, decorative chimneys. A mixture of brick and wood is common. Windows often have one large single-paned bottom sash and small panes in the upper sash. Example: 401 Red River Road, Page 17	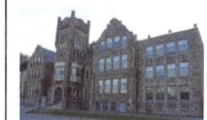

Renaissance Revival, 1870-1910 - The Renaissance Palazzo was a three or four storey building with a rusticated (very large masonry blocks with deep joints and decorated with rough or bold finishes) ground floor, and regularized understated windows on two upper levels, always finished by an elaborate cornice. The Renaissance saw the development of a graceful and balanced adaptation of the Greek styles. In Ontario, the Renaissance was revived in commercial buildings, banks, offices, and churches in many towns. Most of the Renaissance Revival buildings are designed without columns while those with columns and pilasters are more ornate. Example: Hogarth Fountain, Page 14	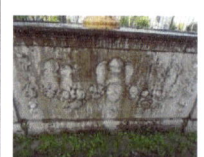
Romanesque Revival, 1880-1910 – This style hearkens back to medieval architecture of the 11th and 12th centuries with a heavy appearance, blocky towers and rounded arches. Example: 294 Red River Road, Page 20	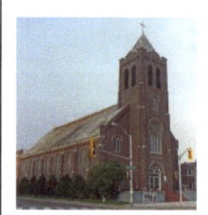
Tudor Revival – exposed timbers with stucco infill, multi-paned windows. Example: 49 College Street, Page 34	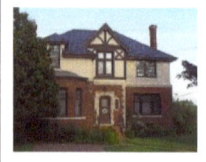

www.ingramcontent.com/pod-product-compliance
Lightning Source LLC
Chambersburg PA
CBHW040242220526
45473CB00001B/340